SOME
LESS KNOWN
WORDS

SOME
LESS KNOWN
WORDS

**A brief dictionary
in larger type**

**Left out are most words an
educated person would know
or ones from special areas
like medicine or biology**

by

Patrick Ellam

www.patrickellam.com

Authors Choice Press
Bloomington

Some Less Known Words
A brief dictionary in larger type

Authors Choice Press
an imprint of iUniverse, Inc.

iUniverse books may be ordered through booksellers or by contacting:

iUniverse
1663 Liberty Drive
Bloomington, IN 47403
www.iuniverse.com
1-800-Authors (1-800-288-4677)

ISBN: 978-1-4620-3500-7 (sc)

Printed in the United States of America

iUniverse rev. date: 08/15/2011

FOR THOSE WITH
LITTLE TIME TO SPARE

A

a bas *French* Down with.

abdominous Corpulent.

abeam *Nautical* At right angles to the keel of a ship.

aberglaube *German* Excessive belief, superstition.

ab initio *Latin* From the beginning.

abjure To renounce.

abnegate Deny oneself (a thing).

ab origine *Latin* From the source or origin.

ab ovo *Latin* From the beginning.

abrogate To repeal or abolish.

abcission Sudden termination.

absently Inattentively.

absit omen *Latin* May my fears not be verified.

absonant Discordant.

absolute alcohol Containing less than one percent of water.

absolute zero *Temperature* Minus 273 degrees Centigrade.

absorbefacient *Latin* Causing absorption.

absorbtivity The ratio between the radiation absorbed by a surface and the total energy that strikes it.

absquatulate Make off, decamp.

abstergent Cleansing.

abstract of title *Law* A short history of the title to a parcel of real estate.

abulia Loss of willpower.

acidie Sloth, torpor, despair.

aby Redeem, pay the penalty of.

academism Traditionalism in art, literature, etc.

a capella *Music* Without instrumental accompaniment, as sung in a chapel.

acaudal Tailless.

acclivity An upward slope.

accretion *Law* Increase of land caused by acts of nature, as by alluvion.

accumbent Reclining.

acentric Having no center.

acephalous Headless, without a leader.

acequia An irrigation ditch.

acescent Turning sour.

acetal Colorless, volatile fluid used as hypnotic or solvent.

acetic Pertaining to vinegar.

a cheval *French* On horseback.

achromatic *Optics* Free from chromatic abberation.

achromic Colorless.

a couvert *French* Under cover.

acre 43,560 square feet.

acronical Ocurring at sunset.

acrophobia Fear of high places.

actinism The property of radiant energy. (like the sun's rays)

producing chemical change.
actionable Liable to a lawsuit.
act of God *Law* A direct, sudden
    and irresistible action of
    natural forces.
actualize To realize in action,
    describe realistically.
actuary One who computes risks
    and rates for insurance.
acuate Sharpened or pointed.
acuity Sharpness, acuteness.
adagio *Music* Slowly, or slow.
ad captandum vulgus *Latin* To
    please the rabble.
adduce To cite as proof or
    instance.
a deux *French* For two.
ad fin *Latin* To the end.
ad hoc *Latin* For this purpose.
ad hominem *Latin* Personal.
adiabatic Without gain or loss
    of heat.
adiathermancy Inability to trans-
    mit radiant heat.
ad infinitum *Latin* Endlessly.
ad interim *Latin* In the meantime.
adipose Fatty.
adit An entrance or passage.
adjudge To pronounce formally.
adjure To request earnestly.
adjuvant Helpful, auxilliary.
ad literam *Latin* To the letter,
    exactly.
admeasure To apportion, assign
    in due shares.
adminicle A help, *Law* Corrob-
    iratory evidence.

ad patres *Latin* To his or her
fathers, dead.

ad rem *Latin* To the matter.

adscititious Supplemental.

adscript *Latin* Written after.

adsorb To gather liquid or gas
on a surface in a condens-
ed layer (like charcoal).

adulterine Counterfeit, illegal.

adumbral Shady or shadowy.

adunc Hooked, curved inward.

adust Scorched, dried up, sun-
burnt, parched.

ad utrumque paratus *Latin* Prep-
ared for either alternative.

ad valorem *Latin* In proportion to the value.

advection Heat transfer by
horizontal air movement.

adventitious Acquired casual-
ly or by accident.

adventuress A woman on the
lookout for a position.

adventurism Defiance of accepted
standards of behaviour.

ad verbum *Latin* To the word,
exactly as the original.

advert Refer (to).

advertent Attentive.

advisement Consultation.

aegis Protection, sponsorship.

aeon An indefinitely long
period of time.

aerialist A trapeze artist.

aerie Nest of a bird of prey.

aerodonetics The study of
gliding or soaring flight.

aerophagia Morbid swallowing
of air, due to neurotic
gastric disturbances.

aerophobia *Psychiatry* A morbid
fear of drafts, gases and
airborne noxious influences.

aerosol Colloidal particles dis-
persed in a gas.

aerostat A balloon or airship.

aery Etherial, lofty.

aesthete A professed appreciator
of the beautiful.

affaire d'honneur *French* A
duel.

affiance To bind by promise
of marriage.

affiant *Law* One who makes an
affadavit.

affiche *French* A poster.

aflated Inspired.

affusion Pouring on liquid.

a fond *French* Thoroughly, fully.

a fortiori *Latin* With stronger
reason, more conclusively.

afreet *Arabian Mythology* A
powerful evil demon.

aft *Nautical* At or toward the
stern of a ship or boat.

afterburner A ramjet at the
exhaust of a jet engine to
give extra thrust.

aftterdamp The gas left in a mine
by a fire or an explosion.

afterglow The glow in the West
after sunset.

afterlight Hindsight.

afterpiece A short piece performed after a play.

agate line Advertising space
1/14th of an inch deep by
one column wide.

agent provocateur *French* Secret
agent hired to provike someone into an illegal action.

agglomerate To collect or
gather into a mass.

aggress To attack first.

agio Allowance for difference
in value of two currencies.

agiotage Speculative dealing
in securities.

aglet A metal tag at the end
of a shoe or boot lace.

agley *Scottish* Askew, awry.

agminate Clustered together.

agnall A hangnail.

agon A contest for a prize.

agonic Not forming an angle.

agonic line The line of no
magnetic variation.

agonistic Combative, polemic,
aiming at effect.

agoraphobia A morbid dread of
public places.

agraphia Inability to write.

agrestic Rural, rustic, uncouth.

agronomy Husbandry.

ahisma *Hindu Scriptures* Non
violence, acclaimed as the
highest form of duty.

aide memoire *French* A memorandum of agreement.

aileron Control surface on wing
of an aircraft that rolls it

to left or right.
air castle A visionary project.
air drain A space below a building to prevent dampness.
airline passengers See E.I.P.,
V.I.P., U.L.P. & R.A.M.
air mass A body of air whose
properties are horizontal-
ly uniform.
air pocket A downward current of
air, causing an aircraft to
lose altitude suddenly.
ait *British* A small island.
alameda A walkway shaded by
poplar trees.
a la mort *French* Half dead.
alate Having wings.
alb A priest's white robe.
albata German silver.
albedo Ratio of light reflected
by a planet or satellite
to that reaching it.
albescent Becoming white.
albumen The white of an egg.
alcade *Spanish* Magistrate.
aldol A colorless fluid used as
a sedative and hypnotic.
aleatory *Law* Depending on a
contingent event.
al fine *Music* To the end.
alforja *Spanish* A leather bag.
al fresco *Italian* In the fresh
air, outdoors.
algophobia *Psychiatry* An abnormal dread of pain.
algor Coldness or chill at the
onset of a fever.

algorithm A way of computing.

alible Nutritive.

alienable Capable of being sold or transferred.

alienist A psychiatrist who specializes in legal evidence.

aliform Wing shaped.

aliment Food, nourishment.

aliquot An integral factor.

aliunde From another place.

allonym Someone else's name used by an author.

allotrope One of several forms of a chemical element.

alluvion *Law* Increase of land on a shore, by the action or recession of water.

almah An Egyptian dancing girl.

alpenglow A red glow seen on the summit of a mountain before sunrise and after sunset.

alpha particle Two protons and two neutrons, emitted by some radioactive materials.

alsib The air route from Montana to Moscow, that passes over Alaska and Siberia.

alter ego *Latin* A second self, a very close friend.

alter idem *Latin* Another that is exactly the same.

amatol An explosive made of TNT and ammonium nitrate.

ammaurosis Loss of sight.

ambages Roundabout ways.

ambit Bounds or extent.

ambry A store room or pantry.
ambsace Both aces (the lowest
    throw at dice), bad luck.
ame damnee *French* A tool, a
    devoted adherent.
ameliorate To make better.
amerce To punish by inflicting
    a discretionary penalty.
amicus curiae *Law* Friend of the
    court (disinterested adviser).
amidin Soluble matter of starch.
amok *Malay* A fit of depression
    followed by an overwhelming
    desire to murder.
amorce *British* Priming charge.
amorphous Shapeless, anomalous.
amor propre *French* Self res-
    pect, self esteem.
ampersand The symbol `&`.
amphibolic Uncertain, ambiguous.
amphigory Nonsensical parody.
ampulaceous Bottle shaped.
ana A collection of information
    about a particular subject.
anabatic Of air going up a slope.
analects Literary gleanings.
anacoluthia Lack of grammatical
    sequence or coherence.
anacreontic Convivial & amatory.
Ananias *Bible* A man who was
    struck dead for lying.
anaphora Repetition of words in
    successive clauses.
anatine Resembling a duck.
aneroid Using no fluid.
anfractuous Circuitous, sinu-
    ous, intricate.

angary *Law* Belligerent's right to seize neutral property and compensate its owners.

angel A financial backer.

angle of attack Angle between a wing of an aircraft and its direction of motion.

angstrom unit A ten millionth of a millimeter (used to measure very short waves).

anguine Like a snake.

animadversion Remark implying censure, criticism.

animatism The attribution of conciousness to inanimate objects.

animism The belief that natural objects have souls.

anion Negatively charged ion.

anisole A fluid used for perfume and killing lice.

anneal To remove internal stress by heating and slowly cooling.

annular Like a ring.

annus mirabilis *Latin* Wonderful year.

anodyne Anything that relieves pain or distress.

anomie A social vacuum.

anonym An assumed name.

anorak A warm jacket with a hood.

anosmia Loss of sense of smell.

anoxia Deficiency of oxygen.

ansate Having a handle.

antedeluvian Belonging to the time before the flood, very old or old fashioned.

ante mortem *Latin* Before death
(as of a confession).

antemundane Before the creation
of the world.

anterior Put before, more to the
front, prior.

anthelion A luminous ring projec-
ted on a cloud or a fog bank
opposite the sun.

anthropoid Resembling man.

anthropomorphosis Transformation
into human form.

antienergistic Acting the opposite way to the energy applied.

antigen A thing that stimulates
production of antibodies.

antilogy A contradiction in terms.

antimonsoon A current of air moving in the opposite direction
to a monsoon and above it.

antinomy A contradiction between
two laws or principles.

antiphlogistic (medecine) Reduc-
ing inflammation.

antiphrasis The use of words in
a sense opposite to their
proper meaning.

antipode An exact opposite.

antiquate To make obsolete, by
something newer and better.

antithesis Opposition, contrast.

antitrade A wind above a trade
wind that blows the oppo-
site way and drops to the
surface beyond it.

antonomasia Substitution of an
epithet for a proper name,

or use of a proper name to
express a general idea.

anxious seat A seat for people
troubled by their concies-
ces at a revival meeting.

a outrance *French* To the death.

apercu *French* A glance, glimpse,
outline or summary.

aperient Laxative.

aphorism A short, pithy saying
about a general truth.

apian Concerning bees.

a pied *French* On foot.

aplantic *Optics* Free of spher-
ical aberration and coma.

aplomb *French* Perpendicularity,
self posession.

apocryphal Of doubtful author-
ship or authenticity.

apodictic Clearly established.

apolaustic Self indulgent.

apophasis Denying the intent to
speak of something, at which
one is hinting.

aposiopesis A sudden stop in the
middle of a sentence, as if
unwilling to continue.

apostasy Abandonment of faith,
principles or party.

apothegm A short, terse saying,
usually instructive.

appanage Perquisite.

appelant *Law* One who appeals to
a higher tribunal.

a priori *Latin* (reasoning) From
cause to effect.

apron A paved area in an airport
    for loading aircraft, etc.
aqua regia One part nitric acid
    to three parts hydrochloric
    acid, it will melt gold.
aquarelle A painting in trans-
    parent water colors.
aqueous Like water.
aquiline Like an eagle.
a quo *Latin* From which (point
    of departure).
arachnid A spider, scorpion, etc.
arbitrage Traffic in secutities
    to take advantage of differ-
    ent prices in other markets.
archetype Original, prototype.
arcuate Curved like a bow.
are A hundredth of a hectare, a
    hundred square meters.
arenaceous Sandy.
arete A sharp mountain ridge.
argil Potter's clay.
argot *French* Jargon, slang of a
    class, especially thieves.
armoire Wardrobe.
armure Woven fabric with ridges.
arraign *Law* To call before a
    court to answer to a charge.
arriere pensee *French* Ulterior
    motive, hidden resrvation.
arrivederci *Italian* Until we
    see each other again.
arrogate To claim without right.
artificer Craftsman, inventor.
artiste *French* A professional
    singer, dancer, etc.
ascendancy Governing or control-

ling, domination.

ascender *Printing* The part of a letter like 'd' that goes up above the rest.

ashlar A squared block of stone for building.

aspect ratio The ratio of the span of an airfoil to its mean chord.

asperse Sprinkle with damaging charges or insinuations.

assault and battery An assault with contact or violence.

assay To examine by trial.

association football Soccer.

astatic Unstable or unsteady.

assumpsit *Law* An action for breach of a simple contract.

astral Starry, stellar.

astringent Stern, severe.

ataraxia A state of tranquility, free from anxiety.

ataxia Loss of coordination of the muscles.

atelier *French* The workshop or studio of an artist.

athermancy The power of stopping radiant heat.

atrabilious Melancholic, hypo-chondriac, acrimonious.

attenuate To make thin.

at this point in time *Bureaucratic Gibberish* Now.

attitudinize Behave affectedly.

aubergine *French* The purple fruit of the eggplant.

au courant *French* Up to date.

au fait *French* Conversant.
auf wiedersehen *German* So long,
    until we meet again.
au naturel *French* Naked.
au revoir *French* (goodbye)
    Until we meet again.
auroral Like the dawn.
ausgleich *German* Compromise.
autarchy Absolute sovereignty,
    self government.
autocrat An absolute ruler,
    with no restriction.
avarice Insatiable greed for
    riches, miserly desire to
    gain and hoard wealth.
avast *Nautical* Stop!
ave etque vale *Latin* Hail and
    Also Farewell.
avidity Eagerness, greediness.
a votre sante *French* To your
    health.
avuncular Of an uncle, or of a
    pawnbroker.
awash Level with the surface of
    the water.
aweigh (an anchor) just clear
    of the bottom.
azan *Mahommedan* The call to
    prayer, from the minaret of
    a mosque, five times a day.

B

babushka A scarf tied under the
    chin, used as a hood.
backdrop The curtain behind the

stage in a theater.

backwardation A percentage paid by a seller of stock for a right to delay delivery.

bad form *British* A breach of good manners.

badinage *French* Light banter.

baff *Golf* To hit the ground in making a stroke.

bagasse Cane or beet refuse from sugar making.

bagman *British* A travelling salesman.

bagnio An oriental prison for slaves, or a brothel.

baguette A gem cut in a long rectangular shape.

bahadur A title of respect appended to a person's name in India (brave, hero).

baignoire *French* A theater box level with the stalls.

bailey Outer wall of castle, or courtyard enclosed by it.

bailiwick The district in which a bailiff has jurisdiction.

bairn *Scottish* A child.

baker's dozen Thirteen.

baksheesh A tip, or a present.

baldachin Canopy over an altar.

baldric A shoulder belt taking the weight of a sword.

balk line *Sports* Starting line.

ball cock A valve operated by a floating ball.

balletomane A ballet enthusiast.

ballonet A compartment for gas

in a balloon or airship.
bally *English* Confounded.
balneal Pertaining to baths.
balustrade A row of balusters
    supporting a rall.
banderole A long narrow flag,
    flown at masthead.
bandog A dog tied or chained.
bandoleer A shoulder belt with
    loops for cartridges.
bank discount Interest on a
    loan deducted in advance.
banshee *Irish* Spirit whose wail
    portends death in a house.
banzai *Japanese* A salutation,
    meaning ten thousand years.
barathrum A pit in Athens where
    criminals were thrown.
barbate Having hairy tufts.
barbecue From *French* Barbe et
    Cue, meaning Beard and Tail.
barcarole A boating song of the
    Venetian gondoliers.
bardolatry Worship of
    Shakespeare.
barge course The part of a
    gable roof that projects
    beyond the end wall.
baric Pertaining to weight.
barker A noisy tout.
barm Froth of yeast, formed on
    fermenting malt liquor.
barmy *British* Full of froth,
    wrong in the head.
barnacles Two pincers, put on a
    horse's nose to quiet him.
barranca *Spanish* A steep

sided ravine, or gorge.

barratry *Law* Vexatious litigation or excitement to it.

barrel house *Jazz* In a rough and crude style.

barrister *English* A counsellor allowed to plead in court.

barrow A castrated male swine.

base level The lowest level to which running water can in theory erode the land.

bashaw An important person, or a bigwig.

basilic Royal and kingly.

basilisk A legendary dragon or serpent, said to kill by its breath or with a look.

basset horn An alto clarinet with a soft tone.

bastion A projecting portion of a fortification.

batfowl To catch birds at night with lights and nets.

bathos Fall from the sublime to the ridiculous.

batik A way of printing cloth, by covering the parts not to be colored with wax.

batiste A fine cotton fabric.

batman A British army officer's soldier-servant.

batracian Of frogs, or animals that discard their tails.

batt A sheet of matted cotton wool, used in bedding.

battue Wholesale slaughter,

bawd A procuress or procurer.

bawdy Obscene, indecent.

beach la mar A form of pidgin (business) English spoken in the Southwest Pacific.

beadhouse An almshouse whose inmates were required to pray for the founder.

beadle An official in British universities who leads and supervises processions.

beadledom A stupid show or exercise of authority.

beadroll *Catholic* A list of people to be prayed for.

beam The width of a ship or boat at the widest point.

beanie A small, brimless hat.

bear leader Travelling companion of a wealthy youth.

beatify Make blissfully happy.

beau geste *French* A display of magnanimity.

beau monde *French* Fashionable society.

beaux arts *French* Fine arts.

beck A beckoning gesture.

bedad *Irish* By Gad.

beer and skittles *British* Drinks and pleasure.

beeswing Second crust on long kept port, or old wine.

beetle Heavy tool for ramming, crushing or beating.

begorra *Irish* By God.

begum Mahommedan woman ruler.

behemoth An enormous creature, probably a hippopotamus.

behoof Use to advantage.

behoove To be incumbent on.

bel Unit to measure power ratios logarithmically.

belay *Nautical* Secure a line to a pin or a cleat.

bel canto A smooth, flowing style of singing.

beleaguer To surround, as with an army.

bel esprit *French* Person of great wit or intellect.

belial The spirit of evil.

belie Give false notion of.

bell To bellow like a stag in rutting time.

belladonna Deadly nightshade.

belles lettres *French* Literature as a fine art.

bell metal An alloy of copper and tin, used for bells.

bellwether A male sheep which leads a flock, usually wearing a bell.

belvedere A building designed to have a fine view.

bench mark A survey point of known elevation.

bench warrant A court warrant to apprehend an offender.

bender *Slang* A drinking spree.

benedick A newly married man.

benefice A church living.

bengaline A fabric like poplin with heavy cords.

benighted Unenlightened.

ben trovato *Italian* Well

invented. Characteristic
even if not true.

berate Scold.

bergschrund *German* Crevasse
at junction of steep upper
slope and glacier or neve.

berm A dirt shoulder, running
beside a road.

bes Egyptian god of pleasure.

besom Bundle of sticks around
a stick, for sweeping.

bestead To help or serve.

beta plus Rather better than
second rate.

bete noire *French* Something
one especially dislikes.

betise *French* Foolish or ill
timed remark or action.

bhang Indian hemp.

bibcock A faucet with a bent
nozzle.

bibelot A small curio or
artistic trinket.

bibulous Addicted to alcohol.

bicameral Having two chambers
(legislative body).

bicron One billionth part
of a meter.

bidable Obedient.

bidarka A sealskin boat used
by Alaskan Eskimos.

bien entendu *French* Of
course.

bienvenu *French* Welcome.

bight A loop of rope.

bijou *French* A small and
elegant jewel or trinket.

bilander A small ship with two
     masts used in Holland.
bilge The bottom of a ship, or
     water that collects there,
     also *Slang* Nonsense.
billabong *Australian* A branch
     of a river that flows away
     from the main stream.
billet doux *French* Love letter.
biotic Pertaining to life.
birdie *Golf* One stroke under
     par for a hole.
bireme Ancient galley, having
     two banks of oars.
birl To spin a floating log
     while standing on it.
bis *French* Repeat.
bisque A point in tennis, or a
     stroke in golf, as odds.
bitts *Nautical* Posts on deck
     for securing lines.
black death Bubonic plague.
black hand Secret society with
     criminal activities.
black lead Graphite.
black maria Vehicle that takes
     prisoners to jail.
blague *French* Humbug.
blimp A balloon with no frame.
     From the early classificat-
     ions: A – Rigid, B – Limp.
blind tiger *Slang* An illegal
     liquor saloon.
blinkard One who blinks often.
blithering *British* Talking non-
     sense (as blithering idiot).
blivet *British* A mythical artill-

ery projectile: Two pounds of
manure in a one pound sack.
bloater A salted, smoked herring.
block letter A type face having
no serifs.
bloody *British* Originally By My
Lady, now used as an adject-
ive, as in Bloody Good.
bludgeon A heavy headed stick.
blue chip A fairly reliable investment, not as secure as a
gilt edged one.
blue sky law One to stop sale of
fraudulent securities.
blunge To mix clay with water.
board foot One foot square and
one inch thick.
bobbinet Machine made cotton net.
bob skate A skate with two paral-
lel runners.
bodega A shop selling wine only.
boffin Scientist, researcher.
bogey *Golf* One stroke above par
for a hole.
bogtrotter A rural Irishman.
bola fazul *Navajo* Bull manure.
bolas *South American* Two or more
heavy balls, with strong cord
between, used as a weapon.
bolid A large, bright meteor.
bollard A post on a ship or quay
for securing lines.
bolo A large, single edged knife.
bolson A mountain rimmed desert
basin with interior drainage.
bolt rope A rope running along
an edge of a sail.

Bombay Where your luggage may be sent if you are rude to a clerk at an airline counter.

bona fide *Latin* In good faith.

boner A foolsih blunder.

bonhomie *French* Geniality.

bon mot *French* Witty saying.

bon ton *French* Good style, the fashionable world.

bonzer *Australian* First rate.

booby hatch Insane asylum, jail.

boomer A large male kangaroo.

boondocks Backwoods.

bootless Unavailing, useless.

boots and saddles *Cavalry* A bugle call to mount.

bordereau *French* Memorandum.

bordello A brothel.

bore A steep tidal wave that goes up some estuaries.

boreal Of the north wind.

borne *French* Narrow minded.

bort Diamond fragments.

bosh *Turkish* Nonsense.

bossy A cow or calf.

bo'sun Petty officer in a ship.

bottomry Lending money to the owner of a ship, with the ship as security.

boudoir *French* A lady's small private room (literally a sulking place).

boulter A long fishing line with many hooks.

bounder *British* An obtrusive and vulgar person.

bourgeois *French* Middle class.

Bourse *French* Stock exchange.
boustrophedon Writing in which
    the lines go from left to
    right, then right to left.
bovine Like an ox, dull.
bowdlerize Expurgate prudishly.
bowler *British* Derby (hat).
bowline A knot making a loop.
box, him got teeth, missy hit
    im, he holler *Pidgin*
    English Piano.
boxing day *British* The first
    weekday after Christmas
    – when gifts are given to
    employees (Xmas boxes).
brassage A charge for coining
    money.
brasserie *French* Beer garden.
brattice Wood or cloth lining
    of air shaft in a mine.
bravado Boasting.
bravo Well done.
bravura Brilliant performance.
break away Start prematurely
    in a race.
breaker A small water barrel.
breakneck Dangerous.
brevet A nominal rank.
brickbat A rocklike missile.
bricole An indirect stroke, in
    tennis or billiards.
bridgeboard Board at side of a
    wooden stair, supporting
    the treads and risers.
brig A two masted, square rig-
    ged sailing ship.
brigantine A two masted sail-

ing ship, square rigged
on the foremast and fore-
and-aft on the main.

brio *Italian* Vivacity.

brioche *French* A sweet roll.

briolette *French* Pear shaped
gem faceted in triangles.

brisance The shattering power
of high explosives.

brise bise *French* A curtain
stretching across the
lower part of a window.

Brobdingnag Land of giants.

brock *British* A badger,
stinking fellow.

brocket A second year stag
with straight horns.

brogue An Irish accent.

brown coal Lignite.

brown shirts Hitler's storm
troopers, Nazis.

brownstone district That of a
well-to-do class.

brown study Serious thought.

bruit Report, rumor.

brut *French* Unsweetened.

B.T.U. British Thermal Unit,
enough heat to raise the
temperature of a pound of
water by one degree F.

bubbler A fountain from which
one drinks without a cup.

bucket shop An investment firm
that speculates illegally
by not executing some of
its customers' orders.

buckram Stiffened cloth for

book binding, etc.

bucksaw Wood saw with a blade across an open frame.

buffo *Italian* A comedy part in an opera, usually bass.

buhl Ornamental inlaid work in brass, tortoise shell, etc.

bulima Morbid hunger.

bulk Structure projecting from the front of a building.

bulkhead An upright partition dividing a ship's cabins or other compartments.

bulla A seal attached to an official document.

bull tongue A kind of plow.

bum boat One selling food, etc. to ships in port.

bumf *British* Toilet paper.

bunco A swindle.

buncombe Insincere speechmaking intended only to please one's constituents.

bunt The baggy part of a fish net, sail, etc.

buran A violent wind storm on the steppes of Russia.

burd *Poetic* A maiden.

bureaucrat An official who works by fixed routine without exercising intelligent judgement.

burgee A swallow tailed flag.

burglar One who burgles - Words like 'burglarized' are just silly nonsense.

burin A tool for engraving.

burke To smother or suppress.
burl A knot in wool or cloth.
burn *Scottish* A brook.
burnoose A hooded Arab cloak.
bursar A treasurer.
burton A light two-block tackle.
bus Short for Ab Autobus *Latin*
    meaning For Everybody.
bushel 8 gallons, dry measure.
buttery A pantry.
by bidder One employed to bid
    at an auction, in order to
    raise the price.
bwana *Swahili* Sir.

C

cabal A secret intrigue.
cabbage Something stolen.
caber *Scottish* A pole or beam.
cable *Nautical* A thich, strong
    rope made by laying three
    ordinary ones together
    with the opposite twist.
cable's length 720 feet.
cablet A cable less than ten
    inches in diameter.
cabochon *French* A gem polished
    but not shaped or faceted.
cabriole A curved, tapering leg
    on furniture.
ca'canny *British* A deliberate
    slowdown by workers.
cachet *French* A distinguishing
    mark, or internal evidence
    of authenticity.

cachinate To laugh loudly.
cacholong A kind of opal.
cachou A pill used by smokers
to sweeten their breath.
cachoucha A Spanish dance.
cacodemon A devil.
cacoethes An irrisistible urge.
cacography Bad handwriting
or spelling.
cacophonous Discordant.
cad *British* One who does not
behave like a gentleman.
cadastral Showing boundaries
and ownership of land.
caddy *British* A small box or
can, usually for tea.
cade (young animal) left by its
mother and raised by hand.
cadre Framework or scheme.
caducity Senility, frailness.
cairn A pyramid of stones as a
memorial or landmark.
caisson A large box with an
open bottom, used to lay
foundations under water.
calaboose *Slang* A jail.
caliginous Misty, dim.
calk To make watertight.
callable Payable on demand.
callboard *Theater* A notice
board for rehersals, etc.
calligraphy Beautiful handwriting.
callipygian Having well shaped
buttocks.
call money Funds available or
loaned on call.

call slip One used in a library to request a book.

calotte A skullcap.

calumet A peace pipe.

calumny A malicious misrepreentation, or slander.

calvities Baldness.

camarilla *Spanish* A group of advisors, cabal or clique.

cambist An expert in exchanges

came A grooved slip of lead as used in lattice windows.

camouflet *French* The cavity formed by a bomb exploded under the ground.

campanile A bell tower.

campanology The study of bells.

canaille *French* The rabble.

canard *French* A false report or hoax (literally a duck).

candent Glowing with heat.

canebrake A thicket of canes.

cannabis Hashish.

cannular Tubular.

canorous Melodious, resonant.

cant hook Lever with a movable hook near the end, used to turn over (cant) logs.

cantina *Spanish* Saloon.

cantle Rear part of a saddle.

cantouchouc Unvulcanized rubber.

capacitance Ratio of change in quantity of electricity to change in potential.

cap-a-pie *French* From head to foot (armed and ready).

capias *Latin* A writ of arrest.

capon A castrated cock.

capot Anglais *French* Condom (little English hat).

capper *Slang* An informer.

capricio *Music* Lively.

capriole An upward leap, by a horse, without advancing.

captious Fond of finding fault.

capybara The largest rodent, up to 4 feet long, found near South American rivers.

carapace The upper shell of a tortoise or crustacean.

carat 200 milligrams.

carboy A large glass bottle for acids, etc.

card To comb with a toothed instrument or wire brush.

careen To turn a ship on her side to clean her bottom.

caret Mark ^ used to show that something is missing.

carillon A set of bells in a tower, played by a keyboard or mechanically.

Carioca *Portuguese* A native of Rio de Janiero.

carking Anxious or troubled.

carminative Curing flatulence.

carom A cannon at billiards..

carpe diem *Latin* Enjoy today.

carpetbagger A banker with no office and hard to find.

carrel A place in a library for individual study.

carte blanche *French* Full discretionary power.

cartomancy Fortune telling
　　with playing cards.
cartwheel A silver dollar.
case To make a reconnaisance
　　before a burglary.
casemate An armored enclosure
　　for guns in a warship.
caseous Like cheese.
cassation Annulment, reversal.
castellan Governor of a castle.
castigate Criticize, or punish.
castle nut One with notched ex-
　　tension for locking pin.
casus belli An incident that
　　justifies going to war.
catachresis Misuse of words.
catbird seat In a position to
　　do whatever you wish.
catchpenny A thing of little
　　use, made for quick sale.
catena *Latin* A chain, or a
　　connected series.
catenary The curve of a chain
　　hanging from two points,
　　not in one vertical line.
catenate To link together.
caterwaul Quarrel like cats.
cathartic Purgative.
cathedra An official chair.
cathexis Adding emotional sig-
　　nificance to something.
catholicon A panacea.
Cataline A profligate polit-
　　ical conspirator.
caudal At or near the tail.
caudle A warm gruel, with
　　spice, sugar and wine,

for invalids.

cause celebre *French* A celebrated legal case.

causerie *French* An informal newspaper article.

causeuse *French* A small sofa for two people.

caveat *Law* A notice to suspend proceedings, until the notifier is heard.

caveat emptor *Latin* Let the buyer beware.

cavil To raise irritating and trivial objections.

cay A small island.

cedilla A mark put under 'c' to show it is sibilant.

cellarage Charges for storage in cellars.

censorious Fault finding, over critical.

centering Temporary framing to support permanent framework under construction.

censesimal Reckoning by hundredths.

centner Fifty kilograms.

centrobaric Pertaining to a center of gravity.

centuple A hundredfold.

ceraceous Waxy.

cerebrate To think.

cere cloth Waxed cloth for wrapping the dead.

cerulean Deep blue, sky blue.

cervine Like deer.

cestode A tapeworm.

Chadband An unctuous hypocrite.

chaffer Haggle, bargain.

chamade *French* Signal for retreat on drum or trumpet.

champaign Level, open country.

champerty *Law* Promoting litigation to get a share of the proceeds.

chance medley *Law* An action mainly, but not entirely, unintentional.

chandelle *French* A sudden climbing turn in an airplane, to gain height.

chandler A dealer in candles, groceries, etc.

changeling Child substituted for another by fairies.

chantage *French* Blackmail.

chaparral A thicket of dwarf evergreen oaks.

chapfallen Dejected.

chapman *British* A peddler.

chargé d'affaires *French* A deputy ambassador.

charivari A mock serenade of discordant noises.

charmeuse *French* A soft and flexible kind of satin.

charnel A repository for dead bodies.

charqui Beef jerky.

chaser An engraver of metal.

chateau A country house.

chatelaine *French* Mistress of an elegant household.

chatoyant Changing in color

or luster.

chatter mark A mark left by a chattering tool.

chauffer *French* A portable stove or furnace.

chauvinism Belligerent devotion to a cause.

chazzan A Jewish cantor.

cheddite A high explosive, noted for its stability.

cheerio *British* Goodbye.

cheeseparing Parsimonious.

chef d'oeuvre *French* One's masterpiece.

chela The claw of a lobster.

cherchez la femme *French* Look for the woman (and also look for the motivation).

chernozem Rich topsoil with lime beneath it.

chersonese A peninsular.

chess A flooring plank of a pontoon bridge.

chesty *Slang* Proud, conceited.

chiaroscuro Treatment of light and shade in painting.

chibouk *Turkish* A long tobacco pipe.

chicanery Legal trickery.

chichi Pretentiously elegant.

chignon A roll of hair worn at the back of the head.

chimera A mythological fire breathing monster.

chimerical Unreal.

Chinese windlass A differential windlass.

Chips A ship's carpenter.
chirography Handwriting.
chiromancy Palmistry.
chitterling Part of the small intestine of a pig.
chivalrous Gallant, honorable, courteous and loyal.
choke coil A coil that allows steady currents to pass but chokes off any rapid fluctuations.
choke damp *Mining* Atmosphere low in oxygen and high in carbon dioxide.
choleric Irascible, angry.
cholesterol A fatty substance found in bile, gallstones, egg yokes, etc.
chop *Pidgin English* Quick.
chorography Systematic analysis of geographic areas.
chose *Law* An article of personal property.
chose jugée *French* A thing that is already settled.
chouse A swindle or trick.
chrestomathy A collection of selected passages.
chromatic Concerning colors.
chronograph. A time recorder.
chuff A rustic.
chukker *Polo* One of the periods of play.
churl A peasant or boor.
chute *Skiing* A steep slope.
cicisbeo *Italian* The recognised gallant of a

married woman.

cl-devant *French* Former.

cilice A garment of haircloth.

Cimmerian Dark, gloomy.

cinerery Of ashes.

cinque *French* The five, at
    dice or cards.

circuitous Roundabout,
    indirect.

circular mil Area of a circle
    with a diameter of 1 mil.

cirque A natural amphitheater.

citadel A fortress to dominate
    the people of a city.

citron A fruit like a lemon
    but larger and less acid.

clambake A bungled rehearsal.

claptrap Language or sentiment
    meant to get applause.

claque *French* People hired to
    applaud in a theater.

clarion Clear and shrill.

classic Of allowed excellence.

clathrate Like a lattice.

clavier The keyboard of a
    musical instrument.

clerisy The learned people.

clevis U-shaped piece of metal
    with a bolt going through
    holes in the two ends, for
    attaching tackle, etc.

clew *Nautical* The lower corner
    of a sail at the after end.

climacteric A crisis, critical.

climactic Concerning a climax.

clink *Slang* Prison.

clinker built Made of boards

or plates that overlap.

clinometer An instrument for measuring slopes.

clinquant In garish finery, glittering with tinsel.

Clio The Muse of history.

clique *French* A small exclusive party, set or coterie.

cloaca *Latin* A sewer.

cloak room *British* Rest room.

clobber *British* Paste used to hide cracks in leather.

cloisonné *French* Enamel work in which colors are separated by metal plates.

clou *French* Point of greatest interest, chief attraction, central idea.

cloudland Dreamland.

clupeoid Like a herring.

coach dog A Dalmatian.

coaction Force or compulsion in restraining or impelling.

coal oil Kerosene.

coaming A raised border around a hatch, etc. in a ship, to keep out water.

coat card *Cards* Face card.

cockabondie Kind of artificial fly used in fishing.

Cockaigne An imaginary land of idleness and luxury.

cockalorum *Slang* A self important little person.

cockatrice A fabulous serpent with a deadly glance.

cocker Indulge, pamper.

cock loft A small upper loft.

cock up *Type* An initial letter much taller than the rest.

cocotte *French* A fashionable prostitute.

coddle To boil gently.

codicil A supplementary addition to a will.

coeval Of the same age.

cofferdam A watertight enclosure used to work below the level of a river, etc.

coffle A train of beasts or slaves, fastened together.

cog To cheat at dice.

cogency Power of proving.

cogitate Ponder, meditate.

cognate Related by birth.

cognition Perception.

cognizance Knowledge.

cognizant Aware.

cognomen A name or nickname.

cognoscente A conoisseur.

cognovit *Law* A defendant's admission, to save expense, that the plaintiff's cause, or part of it, is just.

cohere Stick together.

coherer A device for detecting radio frequency energy.

cohort A group of people.

coign A projecting corner.

coition Sexual intercourse.

cokers Mountain people of West Virginia and Pennsylvania.

col A saddle or pass in a mountain chain.

colcannon *Irish* A stew made of cabbage and potatoes.

coleslaw A salad of finely sliced cabbage.

colic Severe griping pains in the abdomen or bowels.

collateral Side by side.

collectanea *Latin* Collected passages, misellany.

college widow A girl in a college town who has received the attention of several successive classes.

colliery Coal mine & buildings.

colligate To bind together.

collimate To adjust the line of sight (of a telescope).

colinear Lying in the same straight line.

collocate To place together or arrange in proper order.

collogue To confer secretly.

collop *British* A slice of meat.

colloquium An informal conference or group discussion.

colloquy A conversation.

collusion A fraudulent secret understanding.

collywobbles *Slang* Rumbling in the intestines.

coloratura *Italian* Florid passages in vocal music.

colporteur A hawker of books.

colter The blade or wheel that cuts the ground in front of a plowshare.

colubrine Like a snake.

colugo The flying lemur.

columbine Like a dove.

comate A companion.

combe *English* A narrow valley or deep hollow.

comber A long, curling wave.

comeatable *Slang* Accessible.

comestible Eatable.

comet seeker A telescope of low power and wide field, used to look for comets.

comfit A sweetmeat.

comity Courtesy, civility.

comme il faut *French* Properly, as it should be.

commensal Eating together, at the same table.

commensurate Having the same measure, proportionate.

commercial paper Negotiable drafts, erc. given in the course of business.

commination A threat of punishment or vengance.

comminute To reduce or divide into small fragments.

commonage The use of a thing in common (eg: a pasture).

common logarithm One using 10 for a base.

commonplace book One in which noteworthy passages, poems, etc. are written.

commove Move violently, excite.

communiqué *French* An official communication.

commutable Exchangeable.

commutation Substituting one thing for another.

comose Hairy.

compeer An equal, comrade, peer or associate.

compellation Manner of adressing a person.

compendium A comprehensive summary of a subject, concise treatise, an epitome.

complainant *Law* One who files a complaint.

complaisant Gracious, obliging, agreeable.

complot A conspiracy

comport To behave.

composite number One divisible by another number.

compositor A typesetter.

compos mentis *Latin* In one's right mind, sane.

compotation Drinking together.

compote Fruit stewed in syrup.

compurgation Clearing from a charge, vindication.

comstockery Overzealous censorship of the fine arts and literature.

con *Nautical* To direct the steering of a ship.

con amore *Italian* With love, zealously.

conatus An effort or striving.

con brio *Music* Vivaciously.

concatenate Link together.

concent A concord of sounds, voices, etc.

concernment Importance.

concert pitch *Music* Slightly higher than ordinary.

concessive Of concussion.

conchiferous Shell bearing.

concierge *French* Doorkeeper.

concinnity Elegance, neatness of literary style.

concomitant Going togethher.

concordance An alphabetical index, as of the Bible.

concretion Coasescence.

concubine A woman who lives with a man without being married to him.

concupiscence Sexual appetite.

condign Adequate.

con dolore *Music* Sorrowfully.

condottiere *Italian* Leader of a troop of mercenaries.

confabulate Chat.

confer *Latin* Compare (often abbreviated to cf.).

configurationism Gestalt pschycology.

confiscable Liable to be confiscated.

conflation The combination of two different texts into a new one.

confute To prove something to be wrong.

congee Dismissal, without ceremony.

congener One of the same kind as another.

conglobate Form into a ball.

conglutinate Stick together.
congruent Suitable.
conium The poison hemlock.
conniption A fit or rage or hysteria.
connote Imply, in addition to a primary meaning.
consanguineous Of the same blood, akin.
conscience clause *Law* One insuring respect for the consciences of the people affected.
consecution Logical sequence.
consentaneous Accordant.
consentient Agreeing.
conservatoire *French* School of music and theater.
consortium Cooperation of several large interests for a common purpose.
consuetude Custom that has legal force.
consumedly Excessively.
conte *French* Short story as a literary composition.
contemn Despise.
conterminous Having a common boundary.
context Parts that precede or follow a passage and fix its meaning.
contiguous Touching.
contrariety Opposition in nature, force or action.
contrite Broken is spirit by a sense of sin.

contretemps *French* Unlucky accident or hitch.

contumaceous Insubordinate, disobedient.

contumely Insulting, contemptuous behaviour.

contuse Injure, as by a blow, without breaking skin.

convenance *French* Conventional propriety.

conventicle A secret or unauthorized meeting.

conventual Of a convent.

conversable Easy to talk to.

conversazione *Italian* A soiree given by a learned or art society.

convivial Of a feast, jovial.

convolve To roll together, or roll up.

cony Dyed rabbit fur.

cooee A signal adopted by Australian colonists from the aborigines.

cooler *Slang* Jail.

coon's age A long time.

cooper A barrel maker.

cootie *Slang* A louse.

co-opt Elect into a body by the votes of existing members.

cop *Slang* To steal.

coparcenary *Law* A special kind of joint ownership.

coper A floating grog shop of North Sea fishers.

coping Top course of masonry in a wall, usually sloping.

coping saw A narrow bladed saw for cutting curves.

coprophagous Feeding on dung.

copse *British* A thicket of bushes or small trees.

copula A thing that connects.

coracle *Welsh* A very small wicker boat covered with watertight material.

coram *Latin* In the presence of.

corbina A game fish of the surf of southern California.

cordillera *Spanish* A chain of mountains.

corespondent *Law* A joint defendant, often in divorce.

corf *British* A small wagon to carry ore, etc. in mines.

coriaceous Like leather.

corkage A hotel's charge for serving wine not theirs.

corker Something that precludes further discussion.

corky Lively, frivolous.

corned Preserved with salt.

corneoud *Latin* Horny.

corn pit An exchange devoted to corn futures.

corn shock A stack of upright cornstalks.

cornucopia Horn of plenty.

cornuted Having horns.

corollary An immediate deduction, natural consequence.

corporeity Materiality.

corposant Corona discharge (St. Elmo's fire).

corps de ballet *French* Dancers
    without solo parts.

corpus delicti *Law* The fact
    that an offense has act-
    ually been committed.

corrigendum *Latin* A thing to
    be corrected.

carroboree *Australian* A large
    or noisy gathering.

corsair A Barbary Coast pirate.

coruscate Sparkle, flash.

corvee An obligation to do work
    without remuneration.

corvine Like a crow.

coryphee *French* A leading
    dancer in a ballet.

cosmoline Grease used to protect
    weapons from the elements.

cosset Pet, pamper.

coster *British* A man who sells
    fruit, fish, etc. from a
    barrow in the street.

costive Constipated.

costrel A flat bottle, suspend-
    ed from the waist.

coterie *French* Circle or set
    of people associated by
    exclusive interests.

cotquean A man who busies him-
    self with women's affairs.

cotton flannel Canton flannel.

couchant (of animals) Lying
    with body resting on legs
    and head raised.

couloir *French* A steep gully
    on a mountain side.

counter jumper *Slang* Salesman.

counterpoison An antidote.

coup de grace *French* A final stroke, a death blow.

coup de main *French* A surprise attack.

coup d'etat *French* A violent or illegal change in government.

coup de theatre *French* A dramatically sudden or sensational act.

coup d'oeil *French* A quick look, or glance.

court card *British* Face card.

courtesan *French* Prostitute.

coute que coute *French* At all costs.

cover crop One planted to protect soil from erosion or weeds until next used.

coverture *Law* The status of a married woman, under the protection and authority of her husband.

covin *Law* Conspiracy.

coxcomb A conceited dandy.

coypu A large South American aquatic rodent, whose fur is called nutria.

coze Chat.

cozen Cheat, defraud, beguile.

c.p. Candlepower.

crackerjack *Slang* Exceptionally fine or expert.

cracksman *Slang* A burglar.

crank *Nautical* Liable to capsize.

crankle Bend, twist.

crap A losing throw in which the total of the two dice is 2, 3 or 12.

crapulent Suffering from the effects of intemperence.

crawl A pen in shallow water for fish, turtles, etc.

create To make a fuss.

creche *French* Day nursery.

credendum An article of faith.

credenza Sideboard, buffet.

creel An angler's fish basket.

creepie *British* A low stool.

creese *Malay* A heavy dagger with a wavy blade.

creme de la creme *French* The very best, the elite.

crepit *British* New, shiny, the opposite of decrepit.

crepuscular Of twilight.

crescive Increasing, growing.

cretaceous Like chalk.

crevasse Deep fissure in ice or breach in a levee.

criminal conversation *Law* illicit intercourse with a married man or woman.

critical angle The angle at which an airplane's wing suddenly develops more drag and less lift.

crock Advice given by a financial expert.

croup The rump of a horse.

croupier Assitant chairman at a public dinner.

crown saw A hollow cylinder with teeth at one end.

crummie A cow with crooked horns.

cruor The part of blood that forms a clot.

crupper A strap from the back of a saddle, looped under a horse's tail.

crural Of the leg.

cruse An earthen pot.

cyrogenics Research into low temperatures.

crypto A person owing secret allegiance to a political creed, etc.

cryptonym A secret name.

cubature Determining the cubic contents of a thing.

cubit The length of a forearm, about 17 to 21 inches.

cucking stool One in which a common scold was strapped, to be pelted by the crowd.

cucumiform Shaped like a cucumber.

cuesta A long low ridge steep on one side and gentle on the other side.

cui bono *Latin* Who profited by it? For what use?

culch An oyster bed.

cul de sac *French* a street closed at one end.

culet A small flat face at the bottom of a brilliant.

cull *Slang* A fool or dupe.

cullet Glass refuse suitable for melting again.

cultrate Knife edged.

cum div With dividend.

cumber To hamper or hinder.

cumshaw *Chinese* A present – meaning grateful thanks.

cumulus A heap or pile.

cuncation Delay.

cuneate Wedge shaped.

cupboard love That inspired by considerations of good feeding.

cupidity Greed of gain.

cup of tea *British* Anything that one likes.

curare Resin from plants that paralyses motor nerves, used to poison arrows.

curé *French* A parish priest.

Curie constant Relates absolute temperature to magnetic susceptibility.

curiosa Term for books, etc about unusual subjects, including pornography.

curmudgeon A churlish or miserly person.

current assets Those readily convertible into cash.

current density The rate of flow of electricity per unit of cross sectional area of a conductor.

current liabilities Those maturing within a year.

currier One who dresses and

colors leather, after
it is tanned.

cursive (writing or printing)
with the letters joined
together.

curtail step The bottom step
of a stairway, when it
is curved at one end.

curtilage *Law* Area attached
to a dwelling house.

curtain lecture A wife's rep-
roof to husband in bed.

curule Pertaining to any high
civic dignitary.

cushy *British* Easy, pleasant.

cuspidor A spitoon.

customable Subject to duties.

custos morom *Latin* A censor
(custodian of morals).

cutaneous Of the skin.

cutpurse A thief.

cwm *Welsh* A valley.

cwt Hundredweight.

cybernetics Study of communic-
ations common to machines
and living organisms.

cyclostomatous Having a circular mouth.

cygnet A young swan.

cy pres *Law* As near as
practicable.

D

da capo *Music* (repeat from)
the beginning.

dacoit One of a band of Indian or Burmese robbers.

dactylology Sign language.

daedal Skillful, inventive.

daff Put aside, waive.

dahabeeyah A Nile sailing boat.

daiquiri A rum drink named for a mine in Venezuela.

dak *East Indies* Mail carried by relays of horsemen.

dalles Sides of a deep ravine or canyon.

damnify *Law* Cause injury to.

damnosa heriditas *Latin* An inheritance that brings more burden than profit.

dap To fish by letting bait bob on the water.

darkle Lie concealed.

dartle Keep on darting.

datum Thing known or granted.

db Decibels.

dead letter A law that has lost its force, though not formally repealed.

deadlight A cover for a porthole in a ship.

deadline A boundary around a prison. beyond which a prisoner may be shot.

death duty *British* A tax on anything inherited.

debouch To emerge from wood or ravine onto open ground.

debt of honor A gambling debt.

decalescence Sudden absorbtion of heat by iron as it passes

a certain temperature.
Decalogue The Ten Commandments.
decibel A unit of power ratio,
one tenth of a bel.
decillion A number followed
by 33 zeros.
decimate Put to death one in ten
(of cowardly soldiers).
deckle edge An untrimmed edge of
handmade paper.
declassé *French* Fallen in class
or social rank.
declinatory Expressing refusal.
decoct To boil a thing in water,
to extract the essence.
decollate To behead.
decollete *Fench* Low necked
(of a garment).
decomplex Having complex parts.
decorticate Remove the bark, or
outer covering.
decree nisi A decree of divorce
that will take effect at a
later time, unless cause to
the contrary is shown.
decrepitate Crackle under heat.
decuman Especially large or powerful (like a tenth wave).
decussate X-shaped.
deep–laid Carefully, cunningly
or secretly made.
de facto *Latin* In fact, whether
by right or not.
defalcation *Law* Fraudulant deficiency of money, owing to a
breach of trust.
defeasance *Law* Rendering null

and void.
defecate To clear of dregs,
    refine, purify.
defenestration Throwing out of
    a window (a way of killing
    political opponents).
defile A narrow passage between
    mountains.
deflagrate To burn suddenly
    and violently.
deforce *Law* To withold by force
    or violence.
degagé *French* Unconstrained.
degauss Neutralize the magnetic
    field of a ship, as a precau-
    tion against magnetic mines.
degression Going down.
deicide The killing of a god.
deictic Demonstrative.
Dei gratia *Latin* By the grace
    of God.
de jure *Latin* By right.
delate Inform against, impeach.
dele *Printing* Delete, omit.
delectation Delight.
deleterious Noxious, physically
    or morally, injurious.
delict *Law* A misdemeanor.
delineavit *Latin* (the person
    named) drew this.
deliquesce To melt away.
delitescent Latent, concealed.
delouse Rid of booby traps.
demand note A bill of exchange
    payable on presentation.
demarche *French* A political
    step or proceedure.

demean To behave or conduct oneself in a specified manner.

dementi *French* Official denial
of rumor, etc.

demesne *Law* Posession of real
property as one's own.

demijohn Bulging, narrow necked
bottle of 3 to 10 gallons,
usually encased in wicker.

demimonde *French* A class of
women, of doubtful reputation and standing.

demirep A woman of doubtful or
compromised reputation.

demission Abdication.

demivolt A half turn, made by a
horse, with forelegs raised.

demodé *French* Out of fashion.

Demogorgon A mysterious and terrible infernal deity.

demotic Popular, vulgar.

demulcent Soothing (medecine).

demurrage A charge for failing
to load or unload a ship or
truck in the time allowed.

demurrer A legal objection to
an opponent's point, even
if it is granted.

demy Size of paper 16 x 21 ins.

dendriform Like a tree.

dene *British* A bare sandy tract
or low sandhill by the sea.

denegation Denial.

dene-hole An artificial cave in
chalk, entered by a vertical
shaft, often 60 feet deep.

denier A unit used to indicate

the fineness of silk, etc.
denizen Inhabitant, occupant.
denouement *French* The final
    solution of the plot, in a
    play or novel.
de novo *Latin* Starting again.
deontology The science of duty.
depilate Remove hair from.
de plano *Law* Out of court.
deplume Pluck.
depone Testify under oath.
depositary One to whom a thing
    is given in trust.
depository Storehouse.
deprecate Plead against.
depredate Prey upon, plunder.
de profundis *Latin* Out of the
    depths (of despair, etc).
depurate Purify, cleanse.
deracinate To tear up by the
    roots, eradicate.
de regle *French* Customary,
    proper.
dereliction Culpable neglect
    (of duty, etc).
de rigeur *French* Required by
    etiquette.
derma The true skin, beneath
    the epidermis.
dernier *French* Last, final.
derry A meaningless refrain
    in some old songs.
dervish A Mahommedan friar
    given to whirling.
descender *Printing* The part
    of a letter like 'p' or
    'q' that goes down below

the rest of the letters.
descendible Transmissible
by inheritance.
descry Catch sight of.
desiderate Regret absence of,
feel to be missing.
desinence Termination.
desipience Silliness.
despumate To skim.
desquamate To come off in
scales.
destructor *British* An
incinerator.
desuetude A state of disuse,
no longer practiced.
detainer *Law* The wrongful
withholding of a thing
that belongs to another.
detent A catch, by removal
of which machinery, etc.
is set working.
detente *French* The cessation
of strained relations, as
between States.
detrition Wearing away by
rubbing.
de trop *French* Not wanted,
in the way, unwelcome.
detrude To thrust away.
detruncate Cut off a part.
Deus vult *Latin* God wills it
(cry of the Crusaders).
deuterogamy Second marriage.
deva *Hindu* God of divinity,
a good spirit.
devisal Contrivance.
devoir *French* An act of duty

or respect.

devolve To transfer a duty or responsibility.

dew point The temperature at which dew forms.

dextral On the right.

dharma (in India) Virtue, right behavour.

dharna (in India) Fasting on someone's doorstep until he does what you want.

dhole Asiatic wild dog.

dhow Arab sailing vessel.

diablerie Devil's business, wild recklessness.

diaconal Of a deacon.

diacritical Distinctive.

diamantiferous Containing diamonds.

dianoetic Pertaining to thought or reasoning.

diarchy Government by two independent authorities.

diathermancy Quality of transmitting radiant heat.

diatribe Bitter criticism.

dibble Instrument for making holes for seeds, etc.

dicephalous Having two heads.

dichlorodiphenyltrichloro-ethane D.D.T.

dichromatic Two colored.

dick *Slang* A detective.

dictum A formal saying.

didactic Having the manner of a teacher.

diddle Cheat, swindle.

dido A prank, an antic.
dielectric Non conducting.
diesinker Engraver of dies.
dies non *Law* Day on which no
    legal business is done.
diet Congress on national or
    international affairs.
diffident Lacking confidence
    in one's own ability.
digamy Second marriage.
digestive biscuit *British* A
    graham cracker.
digger *Australian* Soldier.
diglot A bilingual book.
dihedral Having two planes.
dilacerate To rend asunder.
dilettante Amateur, dabbler.
diluvial Of a flood.
dime novel A melodramatic
    story for people of
    juvenile intelligence.
dimediate Divide into halves.
dinghy A small rowing boat.
dingo A wild Australian dog.
dinkum *Australian* Genuine.
dioestrum The period between
    the rutting periods.
diopter The refractive power
    of a lens whose focal
    length is one meter.
dipsomania A morbid craving
    for alcohol.
diriment Nullifying.
disaccustom To cause to lose
    a habit.
disafforest To reduce from the
    legal status of a forest to

that of common land.

disannul To make void.

disapprobation Disaproval.

disbosom To reveal, confess.

discept To dispute.

discerptible Divisible.

discobolus A discus thrower.

discomfit Defeat, thwart.

discommode Put to inconvenience.

discovert *Law* (of a woman) Not under the protection of a husband.

discursive Rambling, digressive.

disenchant Disillusion.

diseur An artist who entertains with monologues.

disparate Essentially different.

dissemble Conceal, disguise.

disseminate To scatter abroad.

dissolute Indifferent to moral restraints, licentious.

distaff side The female side of a family.

distal Away from the point of attachment, terminal.

distingué *French* Having an air of distinction.

distrain *Law* To seize goods to compel a person to pay rent or other money due.

distrait *French* Absent minded, not attending.

disutility Causing inconvenience or harm, injuriousness.

diva A great woman singer.

divagate Stray, digress.

divers Several, sundry.

divertissement *French* A short
ballet, etc. between the
acts of a play.

divot *Golf* A piece of turf cut
out in making a stroke.

divulgate To make publicly
known, publish.

divulsion Violent separation.

dixit *Latin* He has said.

doctrinaire A pedantic theorist.

dog days July 3rd to August 11th.

dogie A motherless calf.

dog watch *Nautical* From 4 to 6
P.M. or from 6 to 8 P.M.

dolce far niente *Italian* Pleasant idleness.

dolose *Legal* Having criminal
intent, deceitful.

donee Recipient of gift.

Doppelganger *German* An apparit-
ional double or counterpart
of a living person.

dormy *Golf* Being in the lead
by as many holes as there
are to be played.

dory A flat bottomed boat with
flaring sides ad high ends.

dos a dos *French* (dancing)
back to back.

dosser A basket for carrying
things on one's back.

dossier A set of documents.

dottle A plug of tobacco left
unsmoked in a pipe.

dotty *British* Crazy.

double entendre *French* A word
or phrase with two meanings,

one often indecent.

double header A railroad train pulled by two engines.

doublure *French* An ornamental lining of a book cover.

douceur *French* Gratuity, bribe.

dour *Scottish* Hard, severe.

dower *Law* The part of a dead husband's property allowed to his widow for life.

downs Open, grass covered, rolling country in England.

downstage *Theater* At or toward the front of the stage.

down under Australia and New Zealand.

dowsing Searching for water with a divining rod.

doxy Beggar's wench, paramour.

doyen The senior member of a body, class or profession.

drab A dirty, untidy woman, slattern, prositiute.

drabble Go splashing through, make dirty and wet.

draconic Like a dragon.

draff Dregs, lees, refuse of malt after brewing.

draft tube The flared passage going down from a water turbine to its tail race.

dragée *French* A sweetmeat, often containing a drug.

dragoman Interpreter (in Persian, Arabic or Turkish).

dragonet A young dragon.

drag sail A sea anchor.

dramatis personnae *Latin* The characters in a play.

dramaturge Playwright.

dramshop Liquor saloon.

drawing card *Theater* An act that can be relied on to attract a large audience.

drawing pin *British* A thumbtack.

drawknife One with handles at both ends, used by drawing across wood, etc.

drawn Eviscerated, as a fowl.

dredge *Cooking* Sprinkle with flour, or other powder.

dressage *French* Specialized training for a horse.

dress circle *Theater* Seats on the first balcony, for people in evening dress.

drey A squirrel's nest.

driblet A small amount.

drift anchor A sea anchor.

drift tube One at constant potential, so that electrons passing through it have no change in velocity.

drivel *British* Childish talk.

droit *French* A legal right or claim.

drop letter One to be delivered by the post office at which it was mailed.

droshky *Russian* A low, four wheeled carriage.

drub Cudgel, thump, belabor.

drummer A travelling salesman.

dryad A nymph of the woods.
dry fog A haze caused mainly by
    dust or smoke.
dry ice Solid carbon dioxide.
D.S. Dal segno *Music* Repeat
    from the mark.
d.t. Delirium tremens, terrify-
    ing delusions and hallucin-
    ations from heavy drinking.
duad A group of two.
dub To put a sound track in a
    different language on a
    motion picture.
dubiety Doubtfulness.
dubitable Doubtful.
ducking stool One in which
    common scolds were tied
    and plunged into water.
dudgeon A feeling of offense
    or resentment.
due bill An acknowledgment of
    debt not payable to order.
duende *Spanish* Magic.
duffer *British* A stupid or
    incompetent person.
dulag *German* Camp for prison-
    ers of war in transit.
dulcify Mollify, appease.
dumpish Dull, stupid.
dunghill A mean, vile place.
dulcet Sweet, soothing.
dun fly *Fishing* An artificial
    fly like the larval stage
    of some real ones.
dunker One who dunks.
dunnage Material put under or
    between cargoes in a ship

to prevent damage by water
or chafing.

dunt Blow given to an airplane
by a vertical air current.

duologue A dramatic piece for
two actors.

duple time *Music* Two beats
to the bar.

durante vita *Latin* During
life.

durbar Indian ruler's court.

duress Restraint, compulsion.

dust cart *British* A garbage
truck.

dust devil A small whirlwind.

Dutch oven A heavy metal pot
used for roasts, etc.

dutiable Subject to duty.

D.V. Deo Volente *Latin* God
willing.

dwarf star One of moderate
size and luminosity, such
as the sun.

dwt. Pennyweight.

dyad A group of two.

dynamometer An instrument for
measuring power.

dynast A ruler, especially a
hereditary one.

dyne Force that acting for one
second will accelerate a
mass of one gram to a velocity of one cm/sec.

dysgenic Exerting a detrimen-
tal effect on the race.

dyslogistic Disapproving,
opprobious.

dysphagia Difficulty in
    swallowing.
dysphoria Anxiety, dissatis-
    faction, restlessness.
dyspnea Difficult breathing.

E

E. & O. E. *British* Errors and
    omissions excepted (used
    in inventories, etc).
eagre *British* A tidal bore.
eardrop An earring with a
    pendant.
earing A line attached to a
    cringle on a sail.
earminded Responding strongly
    to auditory stumuli.
earnest money That given to
    bind a contract.
ear shell Abalone.
earthshine Sunlight reflected
    by the earth and seen on
    a dark part of the moon.
easeful Comfortable, peaceful.
easement *Law* A person's right
    to use another's land.
eau *French* Water.
eau de vie *French* Brandy.
ebullience Boiling over.
ecce signum *Latin* Behold the
    sign (or the proof).
ecdysiast Strip tease dancer.
echinate Bristly, spiny.
echoism Onomatopeia.

eclairissement *French* An
   explanation.
eclat *French* Conspicuous
   success, general applause.
eclectic Selecting from various sources.
eclogue A short poem.
ecru *French* The color of
   unbleached linen.
ectype A copy.
ecumenical General, universal.
edacious Devouring, voracious.
edacity Good appetite.
edaphic Due to soil or topography rather than climate.
edict An order proclaimed by
   any authority.
edify Benefit spiritually,
   improve morally.
educe To bring out, develop.
effable Utterable.
effendi *Turkish* Title given
   to a government official.
effete Exhausted, worn out.
efficacious Producing the
   desired effect.
efloresce Burst into bloom.
effluence Outward flow.
effluvium A slight exhalation
   of noxious vapor.
effulgent Radiant.
effusive Exuberant, unduly
   demonstrative.
eft The common newt, in its
   land stage.
egalitarian Asserting that
   all people are equal.

egest To discharge (the opposite of ingest).

egoism Pure selfishness.

egotism Talking too much about oneself.

egregious Remarkably or extraordinary flagrant.

egress Going out.

eidetic imagery A vivid and persistent type.

eidolon Spectre, phantom.

E.I.P. *Airline* Extreemly Important People (see V.I.P., U.L.P. & R.A.M.).

eisteddfod Congress of Welsh bards and minstrels.

ejaculate To utter suddenly.

EKG Electrocardiogram.

elan *French* Vivacity, dash.

eldest hand *Cards* The player on the dealer's left.

electroencephalogram A record of electrical potentials found in a brain.

electrolyte A conducting medium in which a flow of electricity is accompanied by movement of matter.

electrolytic dissociation The separation of a molecule of an electrolyte into its constituent atoms.

eleemosynary Of charity.

elegit *Law* A writ against a debtor's goods or property held by a creditor until the debt is paid.

elegy A song of lamentation (especially for the dead).

elenchus Logical refutation.

elicit To draw forth.

elide To omit (a vowel or syllable) in pronounciation.

elite *French* The very best.

elixir A preparation for changing base metals into gold, or for prolonging life.

ell A length of 45 inches (in England and her colonies).

eloge *French* A discourse in honor of dead person.

eloign To go away.

elucidate Throw light on, explain.

elude To escape adroitly from (blow, person, etc.).

elusive Hard to grasp.

elutriate To purify by washing and straining.

elver A young eel.

emarginate Notched at the margin.

embattle Prepare for battle.

embay To surround or envelop.

emblements *Law* Profits of sown land.

embog Plunge into a bog.

embolism Intercalation (as a day in a year).

embonpoint *French* Plumpness.

embosom To embrace.

embouchure *French* The mouth of a river, the opening of a valley into a plain.

embower Cover with foliage.
embranchment Branching out.
embrocate To rub with
    ointment.
embusque *French* One who
    escapes active duty in
    armed forces by getting
    assigned to a base.
emerge To come up out of
    a liquid.
emersion The act of emerging.
emesis Vomiting.
emeute *French* Popular rising.
E.M.F. Electromotive force.
emigré *French* An emigrant.
eminence grise *French* A con-
    fidential agent, who exer-
    cises power unofficially.
emir Arab prince or governor.
emissivity The relative abil-
    ity of a surface to emit
    radiant energy.
emolument Salary.
empathy Understanding.
empennage The tail part of an
    airplane, including the
    elevator and rudder.
empery Domain of an emperor.
empirical Derived from exper-
    ience or experiment.
empressement *French* Display
    of cordiality.
empurple Make purple.
empyrean The highest heaven,
    supposed to contain the
    pure element of fire.
emunctory Of nose blowing.

ENA   72

enabling act An act enabling a
person or corporation to do
something otherwise illegal.
enactory *Law* Pertaining to an
enactment which creates new
rights and obligations.
en ami *French* As a friend.
enamour To inflame with love.
en avant *French* Forward, or
onward.
en bloc *French* In a lump,
wholesale.
encaenie Dedication festival.
encarnalize To invest with a
carnal form.
enceinte *French* Pregnant.
enchain Chain up, hold fast
(attention, emotions).
en clair *French* (A message)
in plain language (not
sent in code).
encomiast Flatterer.
encomium Formal or high flown
praise.
encompass Surround.
encrimson To make crimson.
encumbrancer *Law* One who
holds an encumbrance.
encyclical A Pope's letter
for wide circulation.
endemic Found only in certain
people or localities.
endermic Acting on the skin.
endocardial Within the heart.
endogamous Marrying within a
tribe or social unit.
endomorph A mineral enclosed

within another.

endue Endow, furnish, put on.

energetics The science of the laws of energy.

energumen Demoniac, fanatic, enthusiast.

enervate To weaken.

enface To write or print on a note, bill, etc.

enfants perdus *French* A rear guard or suicide squad.

enfant terrible *French* An indiscreet and irresponsible person.

enfeoff Invest with a fief.

en fete *French* Having, or dressed for, a holiday.

enfilade Fire from guns that sweeps a line of men from end to end.

en garcon *French* As a bachelor, unmarried.

engender Cause, produce.

engird Encircle, encompass.

engorge Devour greedily.

enigma A riddle, a puzzling person or thing.

en masse *French* In a mass, all together.

enmesh Entangle.

enead A set of nine (books, points, people, etc.).

ennui *French* Mental weariness caused by lack of occupation or interest.

enounce Declare, proclaim.

en passant *French* By the way.

en rapport *French* In sympathy, in agreement.

en regle *French* In due form.

enroot To fix by the root.

ensanguine To cover with blood.

ensemble *French* The whole thing, the general effect.

ensconce Establish (in secret, safe or snug place).

enshroud Cover completely, hide from view.

ensile To preserve (green fodder) in a silo.

ensoul Endow with a soul.

en suite *French* In succession.

entasis The slight convexity of a column shaft (to correct the illusion of concavity).

entelechy Realization, the becoming or being actual of what was potential.

entellus The sacred Indian bearded monkey.

entente *French* Understanding.

enthetic Introduced from without.

enthymeme A syllogism in which one premise is suppressed.

entity A thing that really exists.

entomology Study of insects.

entourage *French* Attendants, surroundings.

entr'acte *French* (performance in) Interval between acts of a play.

entrechat *Dancing* Crossing the

feet while in the air.
entree *French* The right or
     privilege of entering.
entremets *French* A side dish.
entre nous *French* Between our-
     selves, confidentially.
entrepreneur *French* A person
     in effective control of a
     commercial undertaking.
entresol *French* A mezzanine.
entropy A measure of the
     unavailable energy in a
     thermodynamic system.
enunciate Express definitely.
enuresis Bed wetting.
envenom Put poison on, or in.
environ Surround.
environs *French* Surrounding
     parts or districts.
eolith A primitive stone
     implement shaped by use.
eon An indefinitely long
     period of time.
epée *French* A sharp pointed
     duelling sword.
epergne Ornament for center
     of dinner table, holding
     flowers and fruit.
ephemeral Short lived.
ephemeris An astronomical
     almanac or table.
ephod A Jewish priestly
     vestment.
epicedium A funeral ode.
epicene Having characteristics
     of both sexes.
epicenter The point from which

the waves of an earthquake
seem to go out.

epicure One who has a refined
taste in food and drink.

epicycle A circle that rolls
around another one.

epideictic Meant for display.

epidermis The outer, nonsens-
itive, layer of skin.

epigone Of a later generation.

epigram A short, witty or
pointed saying.

epigraph An inscription.

epilogue Concluding part of a
book or a play.

epispastic Causing a blister.

epistaxis Bleeding through
the nose.

epistemology *Philosophy* The
study of the nature and
limits of human knowledge.

epithalamium Song or poem in
honor of bride and groom.

epitome A summary, abstract,
condensed account.

eponym One whose name is
given to a people, place
or institution.

equilibriate To balance evenly.

equilibrist A rope walker.

equine Of a horse.

equinoctial line The celestial
equator.

equipage Requisites for an
undertaking.

equipoise Equilibrium.

equipollent Equal in power.

equiponderate Counterbalance.
equirotal Having wheels all
    of the same size.
equitation Horsemanship.
equivocal Ambiguous.
equivoque Ambiguity, pun.
eradition Radiation.
Erebus *Greek Mythology* Place
    of darkness between earth
    and Hades.
eremite A religious solitary.
erg Unit of work or energy.
ergo *Latin* Therefore.
erinaceous Like a hedgehog.
eristic (argument) Aiming at
    victory rather than truth.
erotomania Melancholy, madness
    arising from love.
erratum An error in writing
    or printing.
errhine Intended to be snuffed
    into the nose.
ersatz *German* A substitute.
erubescent Reddening, blushing.
eruct To belch.
erudition Acquired knowledge.
erumpent Bursting forth.
erythrism Abnormal redness.
escadrille *French* Squadron.
escalade Scaling with ladders.
escargot *French* A snail.
eschatology Doctrine of death,
    judgement, heaven and hell.
escheat Confiscate.
esclandre *French* Scandal,
    disturbance.
esculent Edible.

esoteric Meant only for the initiated.

espalier *French* Framework or trellis, on which trees or shrubs are trained.

espial The act of spying.

espieglerie Roguishness.

esprit *French* Sprightliness.

esse *Latin* Being, existence.

estaminet *French* Cafe selling wine, beer and coffee.

estivate To spend the summer.

estop *Law* To prevent.

estovers Things allowed by law (wood to a tenant, alimony to a former wife).

estray *Law* A domestic animal wandering, with no owner.

estuarine Found in estuaries.

esurient Hungry or greedy.

etagere *French* A set of open shelves for ornaments.

et seq *Latin* And the following.

etui *French* A small case for needles, et cetera.

etymology The study of historical linguistic change.

eudemonia Happiness, welfare.

eugenic Of the production of fine offspring.

eupepsia Good digestion.

euphony Pleasing sound.

euphoria A feeling of wellbeing.

eurhythmic In or of harmonious proportion.

eutaxy Good or right order.

euthenics The science of imp-

ꞁoving the environment.
evanesce To fade away.
evection An inequality in the
    moon's motion, caused by
    the attraction of the sun.
eventuate Turn out, result.
evert Turn inside out.
evince To show or indicate.
eviscerate To disembowel.
evulsion Forcible extraction.
exanimate Dead.
ex animo *Latin* From the heart,
    sincerely.
ex cathedra *Latin* From the
    seat of authority.
excaudate Tailless.
excelsior Soft wood shavings
    used for packing.
excipient A virtually inert
    substance, used as vehicle
    for an active medicime.
exclave Part of a country that
    is separated from it and
    surrounded by others.
excogitate Think out, contrive.
excoriate Remove the skin from.
exculpate Free from blame.
excurrent Running out.
excursus A detailed discussion
    of some point in a book.
execrate To abhor, abominate.
executant Performer.
ex div Without dividend.
exegesis A critical explanation
    or interpretation.
e.g. exempli gratia *Latin*
    For example.

exercitation Practice, training.
exeunt *Theater* They go out.
exfoliate Come off in scales.
exigent Urgent, pressing.
exiguous Scanty, small, slender.
ex lib Ex libris *Latin* From
the books of.
exodontia Extraction of teeth.
ex officio *Latin* In virtue of
one's office or position.
egogamy The custom of marrying
outside one's group.
exorable Able to be persuaded
or moved by entreaty.
exordium A beginning.
exoteric Intelligible to the
general public.
ex parte *Latin* In the interest
of one side only.
expatiate To speak or write cop-
iously (on a subject).
expectorate To spit.
experiential From experience.
expiate To atone, make amends.
exponible Requiring exposition.
exposé *French* A statement of
facts, an exposure (of a
discreditable thing).
expunge Erase, omit.
expurgate To cleanse or purge.
excind Cut out, excise.
exsiccate Dry up, drain dry.
extempore Without preparation.
extensometer A device to measure
small amounts of expansion.
extenuate To lesson seeming
guilt by a partial excuse.

extern *British* A person con-
    nected with an institution
    but not living there.
exteroceptor A sense organ (as
    the nose or ears).
extirpate Root out, destroy.
extravagate Wander away, exceed
    due bounds.
extricate Disentangle, release.
extrinsic Lying outside, not
    inherent or essential.
eyas A nestling.
eyeservant One who only does his
    (or her) duty when watched
    by his (or her) employer.
eyra Jaguarundi.

F

fabricant An artisan.
facer *British* A great and
    sudden difficulty.
facetiae Pleasantries, witti-
    cisms (also humorous or
    obscene books).
facies General appearance.
facilorous Atrociously wicked.
factious Inclined to act for
    the benefit of a party.
factoring Buying and collecting
    accounts receivable.
factotum A man of all work.
facture Making something.
faculative Permissive, opt-
    ional, contingent.

fahlband Rock impregnated
     with metallic sulphides.
faineant *French* An idle,
     inactive (official).
faints Impure spirit coming
     over at the beginning and
     end of distillation.
fairing An external cover
     over part of an airplane
     to reduce drag.
fairy ring A circle on grass
     formed by certain fungi.
fait accompli *French* A thing
     already done and no longer
     worth arguing about.
fake *Nautical* One ring of a
     coiled cable or hawser.
falbala Flounce, trimming.
falcongentle A female falcon.
fallal A piece of finery.
famulus A magician's attendant.
fanciness Without imagination.
fan delta An alluvial cone,
     partially submerged.
fanfaronade Arrogant talk, brag.
fangle Fashion.
fantast A visionary.
fantoccini *Italian* Puppet show.
farad Unit of capacitance.
faradic Pertaining to induction.
farceur *French* A joker.
farci *French* Stuffed.
farinaceous Made of flour.
farouche *French* Sullen, shy.
farrago Medley, hodgepodge.
farrow Not pregnant.
fascicle A small bundle.

fastigate With a conical or
　　tapering outline.
Fata Morgana *Italian* A mirage
　　attributed to fairies.
fat cat Rich person, from whom
　　large political campaign
　　contributions are expected.
Fates Three godesses of destiny.
　　Clotho spins the thread of
　　life, Lachesis measures it
　　and Atropos severs it.
Father Christmas *British* Santa
　　Claus.
fathom Six feet.
fatidic Prophetic.
fatling A young animal, fat-
　　tened for slaughter.
faubourg *French* A suburb.
fauteuil *French* An armchair.
faux pas *French* A false step.
faveolate Honeycombed, pitted.
favonian Of the west wind.
fay To fit together closely.
feathering Delicate use of a
　　violin bow.
feather weighted (race horse)
　　given the least weight by
　　a handicapper.
feaze To unravel.
febricity Feverishness.
fecit *Latin* He or she made
　　this (usually a picture).
feckless Ineffective, feeble.
feculent Turbid, fetid.
fecund Prolific, fertile.
feist A small dog.
felicific Making happy.

felicitous Apt, appropriate.
feline Of the cat family.
fell Fierce, destructive.
felloe The rim of a wheel.
felo de se *Latin* Suicide.
felucca Small Mediterranean
coasting vessel, with
lateen sails and oars.
feme couvert *Law* A married
(protected) woman.
fen *British* A marsh.
feracious Fruitful.
feral Wild, untamed.
fer de lance A large and very
venomous snake, of trop-
ical South America.
fermi A small unit of length
(10 to the -13 cms).
ferret Narrow silk or cotton
tape used for binding.
ferriage Coneyance by, charge
for using, a ferry.
ferrule A metal cap on the end
of a stick or a tube.
festina lente *Latin* Make
haste slowly.
festoon cloud Mammato cumulus.
fete champetre *French* An out-
door fete, garden party.
fetid Stinking.
fetor A stench.
feuilleton *French* A part of a
newspaper, devoted to fiction, criticism, etc.
fey *Scottish* Fated to die.
fibril A small fiber.
fichu *French* A woman's small

triangular shawl.
fideicommissum *Law* A request
that an heir give a part of
an estate to another.
fiducial *Physics* Accepted as a
basis of comparison.
fieri facias *Law* Writ to sheriff to execute a judgement.
figuline A piece of pottery.
figurant Ballet dancer who only
performs in figures.
filial Of a son or daughter.
filled milk Milk with a substitute for the butterfat.
fils *French* Son.
finis *Latin* The end.
fink A strike breaker.
fipple *Music* A plug stopping
the upper end of a pipe.
firedamp An explosive gas that
can form in a coal mine.
firedog An andiron.
first water The highest degree
of fineness in a diamond
or other precious stone.
fishybacking The transporting
of loaded truck trailers
by barges, ferries, etc.
fizgig A giddy, flirtatious
young woman.
flagitious Deeply criminal,
atrocious, wicked.
flagrante delicto *Law* While a
crime is being committed.
flake A frame for drying fish.
flaps Hinged areas on the trailing edges of airplane wings

lowered for slow flight.

flat knot A reef knot.

flavescent Turning yellow.

flaw Wind squall, short storm.

fledermaus *German* A bat.

fleshings Flesh colored tights.

fletch The feathers on an arrow.

flexuous Full of curves.

flinders *Norwegian* Splinters.

flitch The side of a hog,
    salted and cured.

fliting Contention.

flog *Slang* To sell.

floriferous Flower bearing.

flubdub Pretentious nonsense.

fluid dram The eighth part of
    a fluid ounce.

flume A trough, full of flowing
    water, for conveying logs.

flump To set down suddenly or
    heavily, flop.

flutter kick Vertical movement
    of legs in swimming.

fluvial Of a river.

fluviatile Peculiar to rivers.

fly *Slang* Smart, sharp.

flyleaf A blank leaf in the
    front or back of a book.

fly loft The part of a theater
    above the stage, into which
    scenery can be raised.

fogdog A bright spot seen
    in a fog bank.

fohn A hot, dry wind in the
    valleys of the Alps.

foliaceous Like a leaf.

fool's gold Iron pyrites.

footle Trifle, play the fool.

footpad A highwayman, with no horse, who robs on foot.

footstall The stirrup of a woman's sidesaddle.

footwall *Mining* The top of a rock stratum, underlying a vein or bed of ore.

footy Poor, worthless, paltry.

foozle To bungle, play clumsily.

fop An exquisite, vain man.

force majeure War, strike, act of God, etc. excusing the fulfilment of a contract.

foreclose To deprive a mortgagor of the right to redeem his property.

fore edge The front, outer edge of a book, opposite the bound edge.

foreland A cape or headland.

forensic Used in courts of law.

foreshore The part of a shore between the high water and low water marks.

forjudge *Law* To expel, exclude or deprive by a judgement.

forspent Tired out.

fortissimo *Music* Very loudly.

fossorial Burrowing.

fougasse *French* An improvised mortar, dug in the ground, filled with stones, etc. and fired by gunpowder.

foudroyant *French* Stunning, dazzling, overwhelming, as if struck by lightning.

fourflusher *Slang* One who
    makes pretentions that he
    can not bear out.
fourgon *French* Luggage van.
fracas A noisy quarrel.
fractious Unruly, peevish.
frail A rush basket, used for
    figs, raisins, etc.
franc tireur *French* A sharp-
    shooter, guerilla fighter.
frangible Breakable.
frap *Nautical* To bind tightly.
frappe *French* Iced. cooled.
Fraulein *German* A young lady.
freighter An aircraft that
    carries freight.
French letter *British* Condom.
French leave Departure without
    permission or notice.
frenetic Frantic, frenzied.
frere *French* Brother.
freshet A flood in a river, due
    to rain or melting snow.
friable Easily crumbled.
fribble Trifle, be frivolous.
frigorific Making cold.
frippery Needless or tawdry
    ornament or dress.
friseur *French* A hairdresser.
frivol *British* To behave
    frivolously.
frizzle To fry bacon, etc. with
    a sputtering noise.
frou-frou *French* Rustling (as
    of women's dresses).
froward Peverse, refractory.
frowzy Dirty, untidy, musty.

fructify To bear fruit.
fructuous Fruitful, profitable.
fry The young of fishes, etc.
FUBAR Fouled Up Beyond All
    Recognition.
fuddle Intoxicate, confuse.
fugleman A soldier put in front
    of others as a model.
Fuhrer *German* Leader.
fulgent Shining, brilliant.
fulgurant Flashing like
    lightning.
fulgurite A tube formed in sand
    or rock by lightning.
fulminate Explode, detonate.
fulmination A violent denunci-
    ation or censure.
fulsome Cloying, excessive,
    disgusting by excess.
fumade Smoked pilchard.
fumarole A hole in a volcano
    from which vapor issues.
fumed (wood) darkened or col-
    ored by ammonia fumes.
funambulist A tightrope walker.
functionary An official.
funicular Of a rope.
furbish Renovate, polish.
furcate Forked.
furl Roll up and tie (a sail).
fusain A fine charcoal, used
    for drawing.
fuselage Body of an airplane.
fusible Able to be melted.
fustigate To cudgel.
fusty Musty, stale smelling.
futhorc The runic alphabet.

f.v. Folio verso *Latin* On
the back of the page.
fyke A bag shaped fish trap.
fylfot A swastika.

G

gabelle A foreign tax.
gaby A simpleton.
gad A goad, to drive cattle.
gaff *British* A cheap place
of amusement.
gaffer *British* An elderly
rustic.
gag up *Slang* To add inter-
polations to an actor's
lines.
gain A notch cut across the
edge of a board, so as
to support another.
gainsay To deny.
galimatias Confused or meaningless talk, rigamarole.
galley west *Colloquial* Out
completely.
gallimaufry A hodgepodge,
jumble, confused medley.
gallipot A small glazed pot
used for medicines.
galluses Suspenders.
galoot A clumsy lout.
galosh A rubber overshoe.
gam A herd of whales.
gamin *French* A neglected
boy, a street Arab.
gamma One microgram.

gamma plus Rather better than third rate.

gammon *British* Deceitful nonsense, humbug.

gamp *British* An umbrella.

gantry Spanning framework, to support railroad signals, cranes, etc.

gaol *British* Jail.

garcon *French* A waiter (literally: boy).

garner A granary.

garnish *Law* To warn, to give notice.

garreteer One living in a garret, especially a poor literary hack.

garotte A device for killing people by strangulation.

garth The open court enclosed by a cloister.

gasconade Extravagant boasting.

gash *British* Spare, extra.

gasper *British* A cigarette.

gastric Of the stomach.

gastronome A judge of cooking.

gat *Slang* A gun, pistol.

gauche *French* Tactless, awkward, clumsy.

gaudy *British* A grand entertainment, annual college dinner.

gauss Unit of induction.

gavage Forced feeding, as of poultry.

gavial An Indian crocodile.

gazehound One that hunts by

sight, rather than scent.

gazetteer A geographical
dictionary.

G.B. Great Britain.

gear To make a factory sub-
servient to another.

gee A command to a horse
to turn right.

gelation Solidification by
cold or freezing.

geld To castrate.

gelid Very cold, icy.

geminate Combined in pairs.

gendarme *French* A soldier
on police duty.

generative Of procreation.

geneva Hollands gin.

genial Of the chin.

genre *French* Kind, style.

genro *Japanese* Elder
statesmen (old men).

gentile Anyone not Jewish.

genuflect Bend the knee
in worship.

geocentric Measured from the
center of the earth.

geodesic Of the geometry of
curved surfaces.

geoid The shape of the earth
if its whole surface
were at mean sea level.

geomancy Divination from the
figure made by a handful
of earth thrown down.

geophagy Eating dirt.

geoponic Agricultural.

geothermal Of the heat

inside the earth.

geratology Study of old age.

gerent Ruler, manager.

gerontocracy Government
  by old men.

gerrymander To manipulate
  unfairly.

gesso Plaster of Paris prep-
  ared for use in painting.

gestalt *German* Form, shape.

Gestapo The secret state police
  of Nazi Germany.

gestic Of bodily motions.

gesundheit *German* Health (used
  as a toast, or said after
  someone sneezes).

giant powder Explosive made of
  nitroglycerin & kieselguhr.

gibbet An upright post with an
  arm, on which the bodies of
  executed people were hung.

gibbous Protruberant, convex.

gig A kind of fish spear.

gigolo *French* A professional
  male dancing partner.

gilbert Unit of magnetomotive
  force (0.7958 ampere turns).

gimcrack Useless ornament.

gingival Of the gums.

girandole A revolving firework.

glace *French* Iced, sugared.

glair White of egg.

gleep A kind of atomic pile.

glengarry A Scottish cap.

glissade To slide down sloping
  ice or snow on one's feet
  with support of an ice ax.

globate Shaped like a globe.

glockenspiel A set of steel bars struck with a hammer, as a musical instrument.

glomerate Compactly clustered.

glonoin Nitroclycerin.

gloriole Auriole, halo.

gloss An explanation inserted in or beside a text.

glossal Of the tongue.

gloze To explain away.

gluteal Of the buttocks.

G.M.T. Greenwich Mean Time.

gnathic Of the jaw.

gnomon The pillar or plate of a sundial, casting a shadow by which time is measured.

gnosis Knowledge of spiritual mysteries.

gnostic Pertaining to knowledge.

gobbledegook Pompous official jargon (like the sounds made by a turkey).

gobbler A male turkey.

go-devil A device run through a pipeline, to clear it of obstructions.

goglet A long necked, porous vessel to keep water cool.

golden buck A Welsh rarebit with a poached egg on it.

golden robin Baltimore oriole.

golden rule Do to others as you wish they do to you.

gondola car A railroad freight car with sides but no top, used for bulk cargo.

gonfalon A banner hung from a cross bar.

goniometer An instrument for measuring solid angles.

good form *British* Good or proper conduct.

googly *Cricket* A bowled ball that swerves one way and breaks the other way.

googol A number followed by a hundred zeros.

gosling A young goose.

Gotham A typical foolish town.

gouache A way of painting in opaque colors ground in water & thickened with gum.

gourami An air breathing, nest building Asiatic fish.

gout *French* Taste.

gowk Cuckoo, halfwit.

goy *Yiddish* A gentile.

grabble To grope.

gracile Gracefully slender.

gracioso A Spanish clown.

gradin One of a series of low steps or tier of seats.

grains A forked fish spear or harpoon.

gramercy Many thanks (from the *French* Grand merci).

grandee A Spanish nobleman of the highest rank.

grangerize To illustrate a book with pictures from others.

graphology Study of handwriting.

graphomania A mania for writing.

gratis *Latin* For nothing.

graupel A snow pellet.

gravamen *Law* The worst part of an accusation.

graver A tool for engraving.

graving dock A dry dock.

grazier *British* One who feeds cattle for market.

grease paint Theatrical makeup.

greatcoat *British* Overcoat.

green room *Theater* A room for actors who are not on stage.

Gresham's law Bad money drives out good money.

grifter Manager of a side show at a circus or fair.

grillage A heavy framework of crossed beams, to spread a load over large area.

grilse A young salmon.

gringo *Spanish* Gibberish.

grippe *French* Influenza.

grisaille Painting in shades of gray, to look like relief.

grizzled Gray haired.

grommet An eyelet or ring.

gross ton 2,240 pounds.

groundage *British* A tax on vessels stopping at a port.

grout Thin fluid mortar.

guide rope One hung down from a balloon, to control its altitude and act as a brake.

guidon A pennant narrowing to a point at the free end.

gurgitation Surging, bubbling motion or sound.

gutbucket *Jazz* Primitive style.

gynarchy Government by a woman.
gyve A shackle or fetter.

H

habile Skillful, dextrous.
habiliment Dress suited to
     an office or occasion.
habilitate Provide money to
     work (a mine).
habitué *French* A frequent
     visitor,
hachures *French* Shading to
     indicate slope on maps.
hacienda *Spanish* Estate,
     country house.
hack *British* A horse let
     out for hire.
hackly Rough, jagged.
hafiz A Mahommedan who knows
     the Koran by heart.
haft The handle of a knife.
haggadah *Jewish* The legend-
     ary part of the Talmud.
hagiocracy Government by a
     body of holy people.
hagridden Worried, tormented
     as by a witch.
haha *French* A sunken fence.
hajj A pilgrimage to Mecca.
Halakah The legal part of
     Jewish literature.
halcyon days Fine, calm days
     at the time of the
     winter solstice.

half eagle A $5 gold coin.
hallmark One certifying the
      purity of gold or silver.
hallucal Of the great toe.
halyard *Nautical* A line
      used to hoist a sail.
hamate Hook shaped.
hamlet A small village.
handsel A gift to bring good
      luck, at the beginning
      of something new.
hangar *French* A shed for
      airplanes.
hangdog Mean, sneaking.
Hansard The reports of British
      Parliamentary debates.
Hanse Guild of merchants.
hard coal Anthracite.
hards The refuse of flax or
      hemp, after combing.
hardy A blacksmith's bar of
      hard iron for cutting.
harem (in an oriental house)
      Quarters for the owner's
      mother, sisters, wives,
      concubines, daughters,
      entertainers & servants.
harmattan A parching winter
      land wind along the west
      coast of Africa.
Harpy A ravenous, filthy mon-
      ster, with a woman's face
      and a bird's body.
hartal Closing of Indian shops
      as a political gesture or
      a mark or morning.
haut ecole *French* Difficult

feats of horsemanship.

haw A command to a horse to turn left.

hawk To offer for sale, peddle.

hawkshaw A detective.

H.C.F. Highest common factor.

headrace The flume leading to a water wheel.

headsman One who beheads condemned people.

headspring The source of a stream, or of anything.

hearsay rule *Law* That which excludes out-of-court statements, oral or written, offered as evidence.

hebdomadal Weekly.

hebetate Make or become dull.

hebetic Of puberty.

hebetude Dullness, lethargy.

hecatomb A great public sacrifice, or slaughter.

hectare About 2.47 acres.

heddles Wires through which warp is passed in a loom.

heeler A servile follower of a political boss.

hegemomy Leadership.

heir presumptive One whose expectation may be defeated by a nearer heir.

hell broth A magical broth for an infernal purpose.

helm *Nautical* Tiller or wheel controlling the rudder.

helminthic Pertaining to worms.

helve *British* Te handle of an

ax, hatchet or hammer.

hemachrome The red coloring matter in blood.

hematothermal Warm blooded.

hendecagon An eleven sided polygon.

hennery A chicken coop.

henry The unit of inductance.

hepatic Of the liver.

heres *Law* An heir.

heresiarch A leader in heresy.

hermeneutic Interpretative.

hermetic Made airtight.

Hesperian Western.

hetaera A female paramour.

heteroclite Exceptional or anomalous.

heterodox Not orthodox.

heteronomy Being under the rule of another.

heuristic Serving to discover.

heveled *British* Well groomed, the opposite of disheveled.

hexagram A figure formed by two equilateral triangles placed concentrically.

hhd Hogshead.

hibernal Of winter.

hic jacet *Latin* Here lies.

hidalgo A Spanish gentleman.

heirocracy Rule by priests.

higgler A huckster or peddlar.

highbinder Member of a secret Chinese society for blackmail and assassination.

hinny Offspring of a stallion and a female donkey.

hipped Having an obsession.
hirundine Like a swallow.
histrionic Of acting.
hoary Gray haired with age.
hock *Slang* Pawn.
hod A trough on a stick, for
    carrying bricks or mortar.
hogan A Navajo house.
hoi polloi *Greek* The rabble.
holograph All written by the
    person indicated.
holystone Soft sandstone used
    for scouring decks.
holy Willie A hyprocritically
    pious person.
hologeneous Of the same kind.
homologate Acknowledge, admit,
    confirm.
homologous Corresponding.
honoris causa *Latin* For the
    sake of honor.
hoolee Hindu festival in honor
    of Krishna & the milkmaids.
hoosegow *Slang* Jail.
hornswoggle *Slang* To swindle.
horologe Time piece, clock.
horrent Bristling.
horripilation Goose flesh due
    to chill or fright,
horsepower 550 foot-pounds
    per second.
hotch pot *Law* Taking shares
    or properties together
    in order to divide them
    equally among recipients.
hotel de ville *French* A
    city hall.

houri A beautiful virgin, in
    Paradise, for each faith-
    ful Mahommedan.
howdah A seat on the back of
    an elephant.
hoyden A boisterous girl.
H.T. High tension.
huarache Mexican sandal,
    woven of leather strips.
hubris *Greek* Insolent pride.
huckster A hawker.
humeral Of the shoulder.
hundredweight 100 pounds.
hutment Encampment of huts.
hydrius Containing water.
hyperbole An exaggerated
    statement not meant to
    be taken literally.
hyperborean One of a race in
    a land of perpetual sun-
    shine and plenty, beyond
    the north wind.
hypersonic Much faster than
    the speed of sound.
hypogeal Underground.
hypothec *Law* A lien on the
    property of a debtor
    without posession of it.
hypothermia Subnormal body
    temperature.

I

iatric Of a physician.
ichnite A fossil footprint.

ichnography The drawing of
ground plans.

icing sugar *British* Powdered
sugar.

iconoclast A breaker of
images.

icosahedron A solid contained
by 20 plane faces.

id The instinctive impulses
of the individual.

I.D.B. Illicit diamond buying.

idem *Latin* The same (as previously mentioned).

id est *Latin* That is.

idler *Railroads* An empty car.

I.F.R. Instrument flight rules.

illation The act of inferring.

imbroglio *Italian* A confused,
complicated situation.

Immelmann turn *Flying* A half
loop and a half roll.

immolate To sacrifice.

immortelle A flower that ret-
ains its color after being
dried (used on graves).

immure Imprison.

impacted Wedged in (as a tooth).

impasto *Italian* Laying on of
color thickly.

impeccant Without sin.

impennate Featherless, wingless.

imperium *Latin* Absolute power.

implode To burst inward.

impolitic Inexpedient.

importunate Persistent or
pressing in solicitation.

imprecate Invoke, call down.

impressario *Italian* Manager of an opera company.

imprest Money advanced, to be used in public business.

imprimatur An official license to print or publish a book.

imprimis *Latin* In the first place.

improbity Dishonesty.

impudicity Immodesty.

impugn Assail by word, call in question, challenge.

impuissant *French* Impotent.

impute Attribute something discreditable to a person.

in absentia *Latin* In or during one's absence.

in aeternum *Latin* Forever.

inamorata *Italian* Lover (fem).

in-and-in Repeatedly within the same stock (as breeding).

inanition Exhaustion from lack of nourishment.

inapposite Not pertinent.

incalescent Increasing in heat.

incarnadine Flesh colored.

incohate Begin, originate.

inchworm A measuring worm.

incipit *Latin* (here) Begins.

incognito *Italian* Having one's identity concealed.

incommensurable Having no standard of comparison.

incommunicado *Spanish* Deprived of communication.

incommutable Unchangeable.

incondite Crude.

incontinent Unable to hold in (secrets, urine, etc.)

incorporeal *Law* Having no material existence.

incubus An evil spirit, said to descend on sleeping people.

inculcate To urge or impress (a fact or idea) persistently.

inculpate Accuse, blame.

incunabula *Latin* The early stages of a thing.

incuse Hammered or stamped in.

indaba *Zulu* Business.

indicia Envelope markings instead of stamps in bulk shipments of mail.

indifferentism Systematic indifference.

indigested Without arrangement or order, not thought out.

indite Put into words, compose.

indurate To make or become hard, callous or unfeeling.

inedited Not published.

ineffable Unutterable.

ineluctable That cannot be escaped from.

inerrable Not likely to err.

in esse *Latin* Existing.

inexpiable Implacable.

inexpugnable Invincible.

in extenso *Latin* At length.

infanta A daughter of the king of Spain or Portugal.

infidel One who does not accept a particular faith.

influent Flowing in.

infra *Latin* Below, lower down.
infra dig *British* Beneath
        one's dignity.
infrangible Unbreakable.
ingeminate Repeat, reiterate.
ingenué *French* An artless girl
        (especially in theater).
ingesta Substances ingested.
inglenook *British* A corner
        by the fire.
ingrate An ungrateful person.
inguinal Of the groin.
ingurgitate Swallow greedily.
inhume To bury, inter.
in loco *Latin* In place.
innerve Invigorate, animate.
innomonate Unnamed.
innutrition Lack of nutrition.
inoculum A substance used in
        an inoculation.
inofficious *Law* Not in ac-
        cordance with moral duty.
inordinate Excessive.
in petto *Italian* Undisclosed.
in posse *Latin* Possibly.
inquiline Animal that lives
        in another's abode.
in rerum natura *Latin* In the
        nature of things.
insensate Unfeeling.
insentient Inanimate.
insessorial Adapted for perch-
        ing (as a bird's foot).
insidious Treacherous, crafty,
        proceeding secretly.
insipience Lack of wisdom.
in situ *Latin* In its

original place.

insolate To expose to the rays of the sun.

insouciant *French* Careless, unconcerned.

inspissate Thicken, condense.

instaturation Renovation, renewal.

insulator Material of very low electrical conductivity.

inswept Tapering at the front or tip.

intaglio *Italian* A design engraved in hard material.

integument Skin, husk, rind or other covering.

intellective Intelligent.

intelligencer Bringer of news, informant, secret agent.

intelligensia Those people who aspire to independent thinking.

intendant Superintendant of a public business.

intendment True meaning as fixed by law.

inter alia *Latin* Among other things.

intercalary Interpolated, interposed, intervening.

interdental Between teeth.

interference drag The extra drag caused by interaction of two aerodynamic units.

interferometer An instrument for measuring the lengths of light waves.

interfluve The higher land
    separating adjacent stream
    valleys.

interfuse Mix, blend.

interlocution Conversation.

interlocutor A man in the middle
    of a line of minstrels, who
    carries on a conversation
    with the end men.

interlunar Between the old moon
    and the new.

intermit Suspend, discontinue.

internecine Mutually destructive.

internist A physician who spec-
    ializes in the diagnosis and
    non-surgical treatment of
    adult diseases.

inter nos *Latin* Between us.

interregnum Period during which a
    state has no normal ruler.

interrelate To bring into
    reciprocal relation.

in terrorem clause One in a will
    stating that a beneficiary who
    starts a will contest shall
    lose his legacy.

interrupted screw One with a
    discontinuous helix.

inter se *Latin* Among themselves.

intersex An individual who dis-
    plays characteristics of both
    the male and female sexes.

intersiderial Interstellar.

interstice An intervening space,
    chink or crevice.

intervale A low lying tract of
    land, between hills.

intestate Dying without having made a will.

intoed Having inwardly turned toes.

in toto *Latin* In all.

intramural Of a single college.

intransigent Uncompromising.

intubate To put a tube into.

intumesce To swell up.

inurbane Discourteous.

inure Accustom, habituate.

inutile Useless.

in vacuo *Latin* In a vacuum.

inveigh To speak violently, rail (against something).

inveigle Entice, seduce.

inveracity Untruthfulness.

inverted commas *British* Quotation marks.

invidious Such as to bring dislike or unpopularity.

involute Involved, intricate, curved spirally.

ipse dixit *Latin* A dogmatic statement resting on bare authority (he said it).

ipso facto *Latin* By that very fact.

iracund Irascible.

irenic Aimed at peace.

ironmonger *British* A dealer in hardware.

irrecusable That must be accepted.

irrefragable Indisputable.

irrefrangible Inviolable.

irruption Violent entry.

isocracy A government in which
all have equal power.

J

jabot An ornamental frill
on a woman's bodice.
jackass A male donkey.
jack pot *Poker* One that ac-
cumulates until a player
opens with a pair of
jacks or better.
Jack Tar A sailor.
jacquerie *French* Rising of
the peasantry.
jactation Boasting
jactitation *Law* Asserting
a false claim, to the
injury of another.
j'adoube *French* I adjust
(used by chess players).
jade An inferior, wearied
or worn out horse.
jag *Slang* As much liquor as
one can carry.
jalousie A blind or shutter
with slats at an angle.
jejune Meager, scanty.
Jellikek The man who started
a car company and named it
for his daughter Mercedes.
je ne sais quoi *French* An
indescribable thing.
jennet A small Spanish horse.
jeremaiad A lamentation, or

doleful complaint.

jerkwater A train not running on the main line.

jess A strap fastened to the leg of a falcon.

jetsam Goods thrown overboard to lighten a vessel in distress.

jeton *French* An inscribed counter or token.

jeu de mots *French* A pun.

jeune premier *French* Juvenile lead (in a play).

jib *British* To hold back or refuse to do something.

jiggered A word used as a substitute for an oath.

jihad A war of Mahommedans against unbelievers.

jimmy A short crowbar used by burglars.

jobation A lengthy reprimand.

jobber A wholesale merchant.

jobbery Making private gains from a public trust.

jocko A chimpanzee.

joey *Australian* A young kangaroo.

john A flush toilet (invented by Sir John Crapper).

joie de vivre *French* The joy of being alive.

jolly boat Ship's work boat.

jongleur *French* An itinerant minstrel.

joss *Pidgin English* Chinese deity or idol.

joule One watt-second.
journeyman Qualified mechanic or artisan, working for another (by the day).
jugal Of the cheek.
jural Pertaining to law.
jussive Expressing a command.

K

k *Pentagonese* Kilobuck, a thousand dollars.
ka *Egyptian* A second spirit supposed to be present in a man or a statue.
kaleyard *Scottish* A kitchen garden.
kamikaze *Japanese* Divine wind.
Kanaka A native Hawaiian.
kaput *German* Done for, broken.
karat A 24th part.
karma Predetermined destiny.
kc Kilocycles.
keck Make a sound as if about to vomit.
keelboat A shallow barge, with a keel, used on rivers.
keelhaul To haul someone under a ship, as a punishment.
keen *Irish* A wailing lament for the dead.
kef *Arabic* The drowsy state produced by bhang, etc.
kelpie *Scottish* Water spirit, usually like a horse.
keratoid Horny.

kerf A cut made by a saw.
kg Kilograms.
kheda *India* An enclosure to
trap wild elephents.
kier A vat in which cloth is
boiled for bleaching.
kill A creek, stream or river.
kirschwasser *German* A spirit
made from wild cherries.
kismet Destiny.
K.I.S.S. Keep it simple, stupid.
Kissinger's law The first
thing you think of is
probably wrong.
kiwi A non flying member of
an Air Force.
knag A knot in wood.
knap To break (flints for
roads) with a hammer.
kookaburra *Australian* The
laughing jackass.
kremlin Citadel of a Russian
town (especially Moscow).
kudos Glory, renown.
KWH Kilowatt Hour.
kyack A kind of knapsack that
can be hung from one side
of a pack animal.

L

labefaction Shaking, weakening,
downfall.
labile Unstable, liable to
change or lapse.

lacerate Tear, Mangle.

laches *Law* Neglect to do a thing at the right time.

lachrymal Of tears.

lactic Of milk.

lacuna Hiatus, blank, empty part, cavity.

lacustrine Of a lake.

lag Send to penal servitude.

laissez faire *French* Abstention from interference with individual actions.

lam A sudden, hasty escape.

lamasery A monastery of lamas.

lambent Moving lightly over a surface (as light or fire).

lambert Unit of brightness, one lumen per square centimeter.

lamé *French* Material with metallic threads interwoven.

laminar flow One in which neighboring layers are not mixed.

lampoon A virulent, scurrilous piece of satire.

lanai *Hawaiian* A veranda.

lanate Woolly.

lancet arch One with an acutely pointed head.

lancinate To tear, rend or stab.

land-poor In need of money while owning unremunerative land.

langsyne *Scottish* Long since.

lapidate To pelt with stones.

lapin *French* Rabbit (fur).

largo *Music* Slow & dignified.

larrikin *Australian* A young street rowdy, or hoodlum.

larrup To thrash.
lascar An East Indian sailor.
laudanum Tincture of opium.
laughing gas Nitrous oxide.
lawine An avelanche.
law merchant Commercial law.
lazaret After part of a ship's
    hold, used for stores.
L.C. Left Center (of a stage).
L.C.M. Least common multiple.
leach Make a liquid percolate
    through a material.
ledger board The horizontal
    part of a fence, or rail.
legato *Music* Smoothly,
    without breaks.
legerdemain *French* Sleight
    of hand, trickery.
legist Person versed in law.
legitim *Law* That part of an
    estate which must be left
    to decedent's relatives.
leister A pronged fish spear.
leman A mistress.
lemma An assumed proposition
    used in argument or proof.
lenitive Soothing, softening.
lenitry Mildness, gentleness.
lentamente *Music* Slowly.
lenticular Of a lens.
lesion Damage, injury.
leveret A young hare.
levigate To reduce to fine,
    smooth powder.
levirate Old custom by which
    a dead man's next of kin
    had to marry his widow.

lex loci *Latin* Local law.

lex talionis *Latin* The law
of retaliation.

li *Chinese* About one third
of a mile.

libidinous Lustful.

libido Emotional craving that
prompts a human activity.

libra *Latin* Pound.

lief Gladly, willingly.

lifer *Slang* One sentenced to
prison for life.

liger The offspring of a
lioness and a tiger.

lighter A boat used to load or
unload ships in a port.

ligneous Woody.

likin *Chinese* Provincial duty
on goods in transit.

limacine Of or like a slug.

limen Minimum nerve excitation
needed to produce sensation.

linch pin Pin through end of an
axle, to keep a wheel on.

linen draper *British* Drygoods
merchant.

line officer *Military* Captain
or lieutenant.

lingua franca Any language used
between different peoples.

lipectomy A surgical operation
to remove unwanted fat.

liquate To separate or purify
(metals) by liquefying.

lis pendens *Law* A pending suit.

lissotrichous *Anthropology*
Having straight hair.

lithoid Stony.
littoral Of or on the shore of a lake, sea or ocean.
live load A temporary load (as of a train on a bridge).
live steam Steam fresh from a boiler, at full pressure.
lixiviate To leach.
Llanfairpwllgwyngyllgogerychwyrn-drobwllllantsysiliogogogoch Name of a village in Wales.
lobo *Spanish* Wolf.
lobscouse *British* A sailor's stew of meat, vegetables and ship's biscuit.
loc cit Loco citato *Latin* In the place, or passage, already mentioned.
locum tenens *British* Temporary replacement (especially for a priest or a doctor).
lodging turn Duty on railway in which the crew sleeps away from home overnight.
loge *French* A box in a theater or an opera house.
loggia *Italian* An open sided gallery or arcade.
logogram A sign representing a word or phrase.
logomachy A dispute about words.
logrolling *Political* Combining with others to help someone, who promises to do the same for each of you.
logy Heavy, sluggish, dull.
longevous Long lived.

long green *Slang* Paper money.
long pig Human meat, when eaten by cannibals.
long ton 2,240 pounds.
loo A game of cards.
lorgnette *French* A pair of eye-glasses on a long handle.
lorry *British* A motor truck.
lough *Irish* A lake.
loup A cloth mask which covers only half the face.
loupe A magnifying glass used by jewelers.
loupgarou *French* A werewolf.
love apple A tomato.
love seat One for two people.
low tension *Electricity* Less than 750 volts.
lubricious Wanton, lewd.
lubricous Slippery.
lucre Gain or money as the object of sordid desire.
lucubrate To work laboriously.
luculent Clear, convincing.
lumen Unit of luminous flux.
luminescence Emission of light not due to incandescence.
lumper A laborer employed in handling cargoes.
lunate Crescent shaped.
lunation The time from one full moon to the next.
lune Line for holding a hawk.
lupine Of a wolf.
lurcher Petty thief, swindler.
lustrum Period of five years.
lutanist A lute player.

luthern A dormer window.
lux International unit of
     illumination (one lumen
     per square meter).
luxate Dislocate.
lycée *French* A secondary
     school run by the state.
lyddite A high explosive made
     of picric acid.
lynean Keen sighted.
lyrist A lyre player.
lysophobia Dread of insanity.

M

macerate To soften by soaking,
     waste away by fasting.
Mach number One relating air
     speed to that of sound.
mackintosh Waterproof material
     of rubber and cloth.
macrurous Long tailed.
macroscopic Big enough to see.
maculate Spotted, stained.
mafia Hostility to the law.
ma foi *French* Really!
magistral (medecine) Made for
     a particular person.
magneton A hypothetical ulti-
     mate magnetic particle,
magnifico A Venetian grandee.
magniloquent Lofty, boastful.
magnum Bottle containing two
     quarts of wine or spirits.
magnum opus *Latin* A person's
     most important work.

magnus hitch *Nautical* A knot like a clove hitch but with one more turn.

Magus An ancient astrologer or charlatan.

mahlstick One used to support the hand of a painter.

mahout Driver of an elephant.

maieutic Of the Socratic mode of inquiry, bringing out ideas latent in the mind.

maigre *French* Containing no flesh or its juices.

maisonette *French* A small house, or apartment.

major domo The man in charge of a great household.

major suit *Bridge* Hearts or spades.

makefast Anything to which a vessel is tied up.

makeready Preparing a form for printing.

Malacca cane One made from a rattan palm.

mala fide *Latin* Bad faith.

mal du pays *French* Home-sickness.

malediction A curse.

malefaction An evil deed.

malefic Malign.

malfeasance *Law* Doing some-thing you should not.

malgre *French* Despite.

malic Of or from apples.

malinger To pretend, produce or protract illness in

order to escape duty.

maltster One who makes malt.

mana An impersonal, supernatural force, concentrated in people or things.

manana *Spanish* Tomorrow, or the indefinuite future.

manatee A sea cow.

manavelins *Nautical* Odd bits of gear and material.

manciple *British* Officer who buys provisions for a college, or institution.

mandate Commission to act for another.

mandrel An axis or spindle to which work is fixed while being turned in a lathe.

mandrill A large, hideous and ferocious baboon.

manege *French* Riding school.

mangel-wurzel *British* Coarse beet used as cattle food.

manometer A pressure gauge for gases or vapors

ma non troppa *Music* But not to excess.

manse Ecclesiastical residence.

manque *French* That might have been but is not.

manteltree The lintel of a fireplace.

mantic Of divination.

mantissa The decimal part of a logarithm.

manumit To release from slavery or servitude.

marc *French* Refuse from pressed fruit.

march Boundary, frontier.

maremma *Italian* Low, marshy country near seashore.

mare's nest An illusory discovery.

margay A small tiger cat.

marplot One who defeats a project by officious interference.

marque *French* Seizure as a way of reprisal.

marquetry Inlaid work.

marrons glacees *French* Chestnuts iced with sugar.

marsh gas Methane.

mary b'long me, him fella no blooda goodala *Pidgin English* My wife is sick.

maser Microwave Amplification by Stimulated Emission of Radiation.

mass defect Difference between the mass of a neucleus and the total mass of its constituent particles.

masse *French* A stroke in billiards made with the cue almost vertical.

massif A compact group of high mountains.

match play *Golf* Where score is reckoned by number of holes won by each side.

mate South American tea, made from holly.

materiel *French* Available
means, stock in trade.
matinee *French* Theater (or
music) in the afternoon.
matrass A long necked glass
vessel for distilling.
matrix The place in which a
thing is developed.
mattock A pickax with a
chisel head as one end
of the head.
mattoid A person who is part
genius and part fool.
matzo Unleavened bread eaten
by Jews at passover.
maunder To talk in a dreamy
or rambling manner.
mauvais quart d'heure *French*
A short but unpleasant
experience or interview
(a bad quarter hour).
Mayday International distress
call (from *French* m'aidez
meaning help me).
mead Alcoholic liquor made of
fermented honey & water.
means test *British* An inquiry
into the incomes of people
on unemployment relief.
megabuck A million dollars.
megrim A severe headache, low
spirits, whim or fancy.
melange *French* Mixture, medley.
melee *French* A mixed fight,
skirmish or lively debate.
meliority Superiority.
melliforous Yielding or

producing honey.

melodeon A small reed organ.

melton A heavy woolen cloth
used for overcoats.

membrum virile *Latin* Penis.

memento mori *Latin* Remember
you must die.

menage *French* A domestic
establishment.

mendacious Lying, untruthful.

Mendel's laws The principles
of heredity.

menhir *Breton* A tall, upright
monumental stone.

mensurable Measurable.

mephitis A noisome stench.

mercantile agency One offering
credit information.

mercer *British* A dealer in
textile fabrics.

merci *French* Thank you.

mercurial Sprightly, volatile.

meretricious Showily attract-
ive, tawdry.

mesne *Law* Intermediate.

meson *Physics* A particle whose
mass is between those of a
proton and an electron.

messaline *French* A thin, soft
silk fabric.

messuage *Law* A dwelling house
with its land, etc.

metage The official measurement
of contents or weight.

metamorphose To transform.

metaphrase Translation (word
for word).

mete A boundrary or limit.
metempirical Beyond or outside
   the field of experience.
meter 39.37 U.S. inches.
methylated spirits Denatured or
   wood alcohol.
metier *French* One's trade,
   profession or line of work.
metric ton 1,000 kilograms
   (about 2,205 pounds).
mezzo *Music* Half, moderately.
Mickey Finn A drink with a
   sleeping drug in it.
microcosm A little world, or
   miniature representation.
microdont Having small teeth.
micron A millionth of a meter.
microwaves Wave lengths of 50
   centimeters to 1 millimeter.
micturate To urinate.
midden Dunghill, refuse heap.
midinette *French* A Parisian
   shop girl.
Midi *French* The south of France.
mien Air, bearing of a person, as
   showing character or mood.
miff Petty quarrel, huff.
mignon *French* Small and
   delicately formed.
mil A thousandth of an inch.
milieu *French* Environment, state
   of life, social surroundings.
militate To have influence.
mill One tenth of a cent.
milliard *British* A thousand mil-
   lions (a tenth of a billion).
millier A thousand kilograms.

milligram A thousandth of a gram.
minatory Menacing, threatening.
mincing Affectedly elegant.
minim A small thing of no
    importance.
minion Favorite child, servant,
    anumal et cetera.
minium *Latin* Red lead.
minor suit *Bridge* Diamonds
    or clubs.
minutia Trifling matters, small
    or trivial details.
mir *Russian* Village community.
misanthrope A hater of mankind.
miscall To call by a wrong name.
miscible That can be mixed.
miscreant Depraved, villainous.
misdemeanor *Law* An offense less
    serious than a felony.
mise A settlement or agreement.
mise en scene *French* A stage
    setting.
misogamy Hatred of marriage.
misogyny Hatred of women.
misology Hatred or reason.
misoneism Hatred of what is new.
mistral A cold northwest wind
    in the south of France.
mite A modest contribution but
    the best one can do.
mithridatize Make proof against
    poision by taking gradually
    increasing doses of it.
mitis A malleable iron.
mittimus *Law* A warrant commit-
    ting someone to prison.
mnemonic To assist the memory.

mock turtle soup A green soup made of meat and seasonings.

modicum *Latin* A small amount.

modus operandi *Latin* Method of operation.

mofette *French* Foul gas that issues from the earth near an extinct volcano.

mohair Fleece of an Angora goat.

Mohs scale A scale of hardness, used in minerology.

moiety *Law* Half.

moil Drudge, toil.

moire Watered fabric.

moll *Slang* A female companion of a thief or gangster.

mollescent Softening.

molto *Music* Very, much.

monandry Having only one husband at a time.

monograph A treatise on a particular subject.

monomania Being irrational on one subject only.

mooncalf A congenital imbecile.

mordacious Given to biting.

morgue *Journalism* A place where reference material is kept.

moschate Smelling musky.

mot juste *French* The exact or most appropriate word.

motte A small patch of woods in prairie land.

moue *French* Pout.

moulin *French* A vertical shaft in a glacier formed by water falling through the ice.

mucid Moldy, musty.

muckle A cudgel to kill fish.

muddler A stick for stirring drinks.

muezzin A Mahommedan crier who calls people to prayer.

mug To assault from behind by locking the forearm around the victim's neck.

mule *French* A heelless slipper.

muliebrity Womanhood.

mullock *Australian* Refuse from mining operations.

multifarious Of great variety.

multure Toll of grain or flour paid to a miller.

mundingus *British* Bad smelling tobacco.

muniment *Law* Document kept as evidence of rights.

murphy *Slang* An Irish potato.

murrey The color of a mulberry.

muscovado Unrefined sugar, got from cane by evaporation.

musette bag A small bag for personal belongings, carried by army officers.

must New wine.

muzhik A Russian peasant.

mythomania Abnormal exaggeration or lying.

N

nacelle The outer casing of an airplane's engine.

nadir Point of heavens directly
under the observer.
napalm A product of naptha-
line and coconut oil.
napiform Turnip shaped.
napoo *British* Vanished, lost
done, finished, no go!
narghile A hookah.
nark *British* A stool pigeon.
narrow gauge *Railroad* Less
than 56 inches.
nascent Beginning to be.
natant Swimming, floating.
natatorium A swimming pool.
nates Buttocks.
natter *British* To chatter idly.
natty Spruce, trim, neat.
nave Central part of a wheel.
navvy *British* Laborer working
on canals or railroads.
n.d. No date.
neap The tongue of a wagon.
neatherd A cowherd.
neb Beak, bill, nose, snout.
nebulize Atomize.
necrolatry Worship of the dead.
necromancy Magic, enchantment.
necrophobia Fear of death.
negatory Denying, negative.
negus *British* Hot sweetened
wine and water.
nekton Free swimming organisms
in oceans or lakes.
neologism The use of new words.
neophyte A converted heathen.
neoteric Recent, newfangled.
nephogram A photograph of a

cloud (or clouds).

ne plus ultra *Latin* No more,
no further, acme.

nervine Of the nerves.

n.e.s. Not elsewhere specified.

nescience Ignorance.

n'est ce pas *French* Isn't it?

net ton A short ton.

neuron A nerve cell.

neve Granular snow, not yet
ice, on a glacier.

nexus Bond, link, connection.

nicktitate Wink.

nide A brood of pheasants.

nidificate To build a nest.

night crawler The common large
earthworm.

nigritude Blackness.

nihil *Latin* Nothing.

nimiety Excess, too much.

n'importe *French* It does
not matter.

nipper *Slang* Handcuffs.

nisi *Law* Unless.

nisus *Latin* Effort.

nitty Full of nits.

nobble To tamper with a race
horse, to stop it winning.

nobby *British* Smart, elegant.

noblesse oblige *French* Privil-
ege entails responsibility.

noddle Head, pate.

nodous Full of knots.

nodus *Latin* A difficult or
intricate situation.

noetic Of the intellect.

nog A small block of wood.

nonage Immaturity.
nonce The time being, the
    present occasion.
nonfeasance *Law* The failure
    to do something.
nonillion 1 + 30 zeros.
non obstante *Latin* Notwith-
    standing.
nonpareil *French* Peerless,
    having no equal.
non possumus *Latin* We cannot.
non sequitur *Latin* It does
    not follow.
non troppo *Music* Not too much.
noria A wheel with buckets on
    it, used to raise water.
normal school One for the edu-
    cation of teachers.
northern lights The aurora
    borealis.
nosology The systematic clas-
    sification of diseases.
nostology Geriatrics.
nostomania An irrisistible
    urge to go home.
Nostradamus A professed seer,
    a prediction-monger.
nostrum A quack medecine.
nous Mind, intellect.
novercal Of a stepmother.
noyade *French* Execution
    by drowning.
nubbly Full of small bumps.
nubilous Cloudy, foggy.
nudum pactum *Latin* A simple
    contract or promise, with
    no consideration.

nugae *Latin* Jests, trifles.
nulla bona Sheriff's state-
     ment that a party has no
     goods to be taken.
nullah Ravine, watercourse.
nullifidian Skeptic, one who
     has no faith, or religion.
numen *Latin* A deity, a divine
     power or spirit.
nuncio The Pope's ambassador
     at a foreign court.
nuncupative *Law* Oral, rather
     than written (as a will).
nyctalopia Night blindness.
mympholepsy Frenzy caused by
     desire of the unattainable.

O

oakum Fiber from old ropes,
     used for caulking.
oast *British* A kiln for
     drying hops.
obbligato *Music* Not to be
     omitted, indispensable.
obelus A mark used to point
     out doubtful or spurious
     words in a manuscript.
obfuscate Stupify, bewilder.
obi *Japanese* A long, broad
     sash worn by women.
obiter dictum *Latin* An in-
     cidental opinion.
oblate (a spheroid) Flatten-
     ed at the poles.
obligor *Law* One who gives a

bond, or is bound.
oblong Elongated.
obloquy Abuse, detraction.
obovate Ovate with the narrow
end at the base.
obscurant One who opposes inquiry or enlightenment.
obsecration Earnest entreaty.
obsequy A funeral rite or
ceremony.
obtest To call to witness.
obtund Blunt, deaden.
obturate Close, seal, stop up.
obverse The front of a thing.
ochlocracy Mob rule.
octavo About 6 x 9 inches.
octroi Tax on certain things
entering a town.
od Power believed to account
for magnetism, mesmerism
and chemical action.
odalisque A female slave in
a harem.
odontalgia Toothache.
odontograph An instrument for
laying out the shapes of
geared teeth or rachets.
oenology Wine making.
oersted Unit of magnetic force.
oestrus A passionate impulse.
officinal (a drug) Kept in
stock by apothecaries.
offprint A reprint of an article from a publication.
off-stage *Theater* Out of the
sight of the audience.
of the profession Theater.

o.g. A stamp with the original
       gum still on it.
ogee A double curve (one way
       and then the other).
oil of vitriol Sulphuric acid.
old-line Conservative.
oleaginous Like oil.
olfaction Smelling.
olio A mixed dish, hotchpotch.
olla podrida *Spanish* A rotten
       pot (incongruous mixture).
omnifarious Of all forms.
omophagia Eating raw food.
oncology Treatment of tumors.
on dit *French* They say.
ondograph Instrument to record
       oscillatory variations.
oneirocritic An interpreter
       of dreams.
on the game Whoring.
onus *Latin* A responsibility.
oom *Dutch* Uncle.
opera bouffé *French* A comic
       or farcical opera.
op.cit. Opere citato *Latin*
       meaning: the work cited.
ophiolatry Serpent worship.
opthalmic Of the eye.
oppilate Block, obstruct.
opprobrium Disgrace incurred
       by shameful conduct.
oppugn To assail by criticism,
       argument or action.
opuscule A small work.
ordinal (number) Defining a
       thing's position in a
       series (as first).

ordonnance Arrangement of
      a thing's parts.
ordure Filth, dung.
organon A system of thought.
oriel A bay window.
orlop Lowest deck in a ship.
ormolu Gilded bronze, used to
      decorate furniture.
ornithopter An aircraft that
      flaps its wings.
ort Scraps of food left at
      a meal, refuse.
orthocenter The point of inter-
      section of the altitudes
      of a triangle.
orthoepy The study of correct
      pronounciation.
orthography Correct spelling.
oscitant Gaping, yawning,
      drowsy, inattentive.
osculate To kiss.
osseous Bony.
ossuary A place for the bones
      of the dead.
oubliette *French* A secret
      shaft, open at the top,
      to drop people into.
ouija board Used by mediums to
      get messages from the dead.
oust *Law* Eject, disposess.
outage A quantity lacking.
outherod To outdo anyone in
      extravagance or excess.
outré *French* Outside the
      bounds of propriety.
overshot (of a water wheel)
      Driven by water passing

over the top of it.

overt Unconcealed.

over the counter (bought or sold) Other than on an exchange.

overweening Conceited, arrogant, presumptious.

ovine Like sheep.

owl train *Railroad* One that runs during the night.

oxymoron A figure of speech with pointed conjunction of contradictions (as in make haste slowly).

P

P.A. Position approximate.

pablum Food.

pace *Latin* With all deference to.

pachyderm Any thick skinned quadruped (elephant, rhinocerous, etc).

pacifico *Spanish* A peaceful person.

packet A boat carrying mail, etc. on a fixed route.

packman A peddler.

padlock law One providing for locking up premises.

paddy Rice in the husk.

padrone *Italian* Employer of street musicians, begging children, etc.

paean Any song of praise,

joy or triumph.
painter A line to fasten a
     boat to a ship or a dock.
painter's colic Lead poisoning.
paladin A heroic champion.
palaver Profuse or idle talk.
pale A stake for a fence,
     a boundary.
palfrey A riding horse.
palindrome A word or phrase
     that reads the same back-
     ward as it does forward.
palinode A recantation.
palliasse *British* A straw
     filled mattress.
palsy Paralysis.
palter To equivocate or trifle.
paludal Of marshes.
panache Display.
pandect Complete body of laws.
pander A pimp.
pandowdy A deep pie made with
     apples and molasses.
panegyric Laudatory.
pansophy Universal wisdom.
pantechnicon *British* A fur-
     niture van.
pantelegraph A facsimile
     telegraph.
pantile A curved roof tile.
pantofle A slipper.
pantograph Device to transfer
     electricity from an over-
     head wire to a vehicle.
panzer *German* Armored.
paradigm Example, pattern.
parallax Apparent displace-

ment of an object, due to
movement of the observer.

paraph Flourish after a signature (to prevent forgery).

paraselene A bright spot on a
luna halo, a mock moon.

parasol *French* A sunshade.

par avion *French* By air mail.

parcenary *Law* Joint heirship.

paregoric A soothing medecine.

par excellence *French* By excellence or superiority.

pari passu *Latin* With equal
pace, side by side.

parity Equality.

parlous Dangerous, very great.

parochial school One run by
a religious organization.

parol *Law* By word of mouth.

parr A young salmon.

parsec About 3.26 light years.

Parthian shot A rearward shot
by a mounted archer.

particeps criminis *Latin* An
accomplice to a crime.

parti pris *French* A decision
taken, foregone conclusion.

parvenu *French* An upstart.

pas du tout *French* Not at all.

pavid Frightened, timid.

pavonine Of or like a peacock.

peag Wampum.

peart Lively, brisk, cheerful.

peccadillo *Spanish* A petty
sin, trifling offense.

peccavi *Latin* I have sinned.

peculate To embezzle (money

entrusted to one's care).

peculium *Latin* Private
property.

pedagogue A schoolteacher.

pedant One who makes a tedious
show of learning.

pedantry Slavish attention to
rules, details, etc.

peddlery The business of a
peddler.

peddling Trifling, paltry.

pederasty Unnatural sex relations between males.

pedicular Lousy.

pedobaptism Baptism of infants.

pedology The study of children.

peel A long handled tool to
move bread in an oven.

peeler *British* A policeman.

peen The wedge shaped or thin
end of a hammer head.

pelage The fur, hair or wool
of a quadruped.

pelagic Of the open sea.

pellucid Transparent, clear.

pelota *Spanish* Jai alai.

peltry Fur kins, pelts.

pemmican Dried, pounded meat,
with melted fat, flavored
with dried fruits.

penannular Almost like a ring.

pence *British* Pennies.

pend To remain undecided,
to hang.

pendente lite *Latin* While
the suit is in progress.

penetralia The innermost parts

or recesses.

penicillate Having a pencil.

penis *Latin* Tail.

pennate Winged, feathered.

penny-a-liner *British* A hack writer.

penny dreadful *British* A dime novel.

penstock A flume taking water to a water wheel.

pent Shut in.

pentad Five years.

pentamerous In five parts.

pentomic Organization of an army division into five units for combat with atomic weapons.

peptic Digestive.

perambulate Walk through, over or about, travel through.

perambulator *British* A baby carriage.

percipient Perceiving.

per contra *Latin* To the other side of an account.

per diem *Latin* By the day.

perdition Damnation.

perdu Hidden or concealed.

perdurable Permanent, eternal.

pere *French* Father.

peregrinate To travel, journey.

perfidy A breach of faith or trust, treachery.

perfunctory Done merely as an uninteresting or routine duty, superficial.

perfuse To cover with color, moisture, et cetera.

peri *Persian* A fairy, a beaut-
　　iful, graceful being.
periapt An amulet.
perigee The point in a planet's
　　orbit nearest to earth.
perihelion Point in a planet's
　　orbit nearest to the sun.
peripatetic Walking or travel-
　　ling about.
periphrasis Circumlocution.
per mensem *Latin* By the month.
permute To alter.
pernicious Destructive, deadly,
　　ruinous, fatal.
pernickety Fastidious, requir-
　　ing careful handling.
peroration The conclusion of a
　　speech, recapitulation.
perquisite Casual profit.
perry *British* Pear cider.
persiflage Bantering talk.
personage A person of distinct-
　　ion or importance.
personal equation Personal tend-
　　ency to deviation or error.
personalty *Law* Personal estate
　　or property.
persona non grata *Latin* An
　　unacceptable person.
perspicacity Keenness of mental
　　perception, penetration.
perspicuity Clearness or lucid-
　　ity (of a statement).
pertinacious Stubborn, persis-
　　tent, obstinate.
pervious Accessible, permeable.
pesthole A location prone to

epidemic disease.
pestilence A fatal epidemic
disease, bubonic plague.
petard *French* An explosive
device, to open a door.
petcock A valve for draining
an engine or radiator.
petit *Law* Small, minor.
petite *French* Small, tiny.
petrifaction The process of
petrifying.
petroglyph A drawing on rock
made by primitive people.
petrol *British* Gasoline.
petroleur *French* An arsonist
who uses petroleum.
pettifog To run a petty or
shifty law business.
petty sessions *British* A
court held before a
justice of the peace.
peu a peu *French* Little
by little.
peu de chose *French* A
small matter.
p.f. *Music* Louder.
phantasm Illusion, phantom.
pharmacopoeia A book listing
drugs and medecines.
phenobarbital An hypnotic.
Philadelphia lawyer One of out-
standing ability with fine
points and technicalities.
philander To make love without
serious intentions.
philanthropy Love of mankind.
philately Stamp collecting.

philharmonic Fond of music.
phillumenist One who collects
    match box labels.
philogyny Love of women.
philology The study of written
    records.
philter A love potion.
phosphene Rings of light caused
    by pressure on eyeball.
phosphoresce To emit light
    without combustion.
phot 1 lumen per sq. cm.
photic Of light.
photogene An afterimage on
    the retina.
photogrammetry Using photogra-
    phs to make surveys & maps.
photokinesis Movement occurring
    on exposure to light.
photolysis The breakdown of mat-
    erials exposed to light.
photophobia Dread of light.
phrenetic Delirious, insane.
physiognomy The face, as an ind-
    ication of character.
piacular Sinful, wicked.
piaffe *French* (of a horse) to
    lift the diagonally opposite
    legs but not go anywhere.
pianissimo *Music* Very softly.
piano *Music* Soft, subdued.
piazza *Italian* A public square
    or market place.
pica A perverted appetite for
    unnatural food.
picaroon Rogue, thief, pirate.
piccalilli A pickle of chopped

vegetables and hot spices.

piceous Like pitch.

pidgin English Business English
- for example: English
words and Chinese grammar.

piece de resistance *French* The
main event of a series.

piece dyed Dyed after weaving.

pied a terre *French* Somewhere
to stay.

pieplant Rhubarb (used in pies).

piezoelectricity That caused by
pressure (as on a crystal).

piezometer An instrument for
measuring pressure.

piggybacking Transporting truck
trailers on railroad cars.

pike *Slang* To go quickly.

pilot balloon One used to check
wind direction and speed
at various altitudes.

pilous Hairlike.

pilule A little pill.

pina *Spanish* Pineapple.

pince nez *French* Eyeglasses
clipped to nose by spring.

pindling Puny, sickly.

pinguid Fat, oily, unctuous.

pink tea *Slang* A stylish or elegant reception or person.

pinnate Like a feather.

pinole *Aztec* Dried, ground and
sweetened corn flour.

pintle A pin or bolt, on which
something turns.

pinxit *Latin* Painted by.

piolet *French* Climber's ice ax.

pip *British* One of the spots
     on dice or playing cards.
pipkin A small earthenware pot.
pirogue A canoe made from the
     hollowed trunk of a tree.
pis aller *French* Last resort.
pisciculture Rearing fish.
piscine Of fishes.
pisé *French* Rammed earth or
     clay, as building material.
pismire An ant.
pithecoid Like an ape.
piton *Climbing* A metal spike
     with an eye for a rope.
pixilated Slightly crazy.
pizzicato *Music* Played by
     plucking strings.
placer *Mining* A deposit con-
     taining particles of gold.
placet *Latin* It pleases me.
     (used in voting).
placket A slit at the top of a
     skirt, used to put it on.
plain laid (rope) Of 3 strands
     with right hand twist.
plaint *Law* Statement of griev-
     ance made to a court.
plaister A braid or plait.
planchet A blank for a coin.
planchette A board on casters,
     and a pencil, said to write
     messages when touched.
Planck's constant Expresses the
     proportion of the energy of
     a wavelike radiation to its
     frequency.
plangent (of sound) Beating,

dashing, moaning.

planimeter Instrument to measure areas of plane figures.

planish Flatten, smooth (metal).

plash To bend & weave branches, so as to form a hedge.

plashy Marshy, wet.

platelet A microscopic disc in blood (aids coagulation).

playa Floor of a desert basin with interior drainage.

pleb A plebeian or commoner.

plectrum Small piece of ivory or metal to pluck strings of a mandolin or guitar.

pledget A small wad of lint to use on a wound.

pledgor *Law* One who deposits property as a pledge.

plenary Entire, absolute, unqualified, full, complete.

plenipotent Having full power.

plenitude Fullness, completeness, abundance.

pleno jure *Latin* With full right.

plenum A container of air, gas or other matter.

pleonasm Redundancy of expression.

Plimsoll line One marking the maximum depth to which a ship may be laden.

plumbago Graphite.

plumbum *Latin* Lead.

plumose Feathered.

plutocracy Rule of the wealthy.

pluvial Of rain, rainy.
pneuma *Greek* The soul, the vital spirit.
pneumatic Of air, or gas.
poco *Music* Somewhat.
pococurante *Italian* A careless or indifferent person.
pogrom *Russian* Organized massacre of a body or class.
pol *Hawaiian* Taro root baked, pounded, moistened and fermented.
pollu *French* A soldier.
point (of a compass) Eleven and a quarter degrees.
point duty *British* Traffic control by a policeman at an intersection.
polder A tract of land taken from the sea, enclosed and protected by dikes.
polemic Controversial, disputatious.
pollard A tree cut back to make a dense mass of branches.
polled Hornless.
polliwog A tadpole.
poltergeist *German* Noisy ghost.
poltroon A spiritless coward.
polyandry Having more than one husband at a time.
polychromatic With many colors.
polyclinic One dealing with various diseases.
polyglot Knowing many languages.
polyhedral Many faced.
polyhistor A person of great and

varied learning.

polymorphous Having many forms.

polynomial Having several names.

polyphagia Voracity.

polytechnic Of various arts.

pomace Crushed apples (in the making of cider).

pomiculture Growing fruit.

pommy A British immigrant to Australia or New Zealand.

ponce *French* A pimp.

pondage Capacity of a pond.

pone Corn bread.

poniard A dagger.

popinjay A vain, chattering person, coxcomb.

poppet A valve that is lifted from its seat (not hinged).

popple (water) Tumble about, toss to and fro.

populace The common people, as distinguished from the upper classes.

porcine Like a pig.

porringer A deep dish for porridge or soup.

port The left side of a boat, facing forward.

portage Carrying a boat from one water to another.

portamento *Music* Gliding from one pitch to another.

Portia A female lawyer.

portmanteau word One made by blending two words, like brunch (breakfast & lunch).

pose To embarrass someone by a

difficult question.

poseur *French* Affected person.

POSH Port outbound, starboard home. The best cabins in a ship to India, assigned to privileged passengers.

positron A positive particle with a mass equal to that of an electron.

posse Men with legal authority to help a peace officer.

postern A back door, side way or entrance.

postil A marginal note.

post mortem *Latin* After death.

post obit Effective after a person's death.

postprandial After dinner.

potable Fit to drink.

potage *French* Soup.

potamic Of streams.

potation Drinking.

pot cheese Cottage cheese.

potpourri *French* A mixture of dried flowers and spices kept for its fragrance.

potter *British* Putter.

poult Young of domestic fowl.

poundal Unit of force.

pourboire *French* A tip.

pourparler *French* An informal preliminary discussion.

pousse-café *French* A small glass of liqueur, served after coffee.

pou sto *Greek* A place to stand, a basis of operation.

praedial Of land, real, landed.

pragmatism Officiousness, pedantry, dogmatism.

praline Nuts browned in sugar.

prank Erratic action (of machinery).

pratique *French* License to use a port, given a ship with a clean bill of health.

praxis Practice (as opposed to theory).

precatory Expressing entreaty.

precept Command, maxim.

preceptor Teacher, instructor.

preciosity Affected refinement.

precisian One who is rigidly precise or punctillious.

preclinical *Medecine* Before the appearance of symptoms.

preconcert Arrange beforehand.

predicate To proclaim, declare, affirm or assert.

predilection Partiality.

preemption The act or right of purchasing before, or in preference to, others.

prehensile Capable of grasping.

prelect To lecture publicly.

prelibation Foretaste.

premise A statement from which another is inferred.

prenotion A preconception.

prepense Deliberate, intentional, premeditated.

prepossess To imbue, inspire or prejudice.

preprint An advance printing.

presage Omen, portent, presentiment, foreboding.

prescience Foreknowledge, foresight.

prescind To separate (in thought), abstract.

prescript Ordinance, law, rule or regulation.

pressmark One put on a book to indicate its location in a library.

pressure head The pressure of fluid at any point in a system, divided by the weight of the fluid.

prestidigitation Sleight of hand, legerdemain.

presto *Music* Quickly.

preterition Omission, isregard, neglect.

prevenient Antecedent.

previse Foresee, forewarn.

pricket A spike on which to stick a candle.

prig *Slang* To steal.

prima facie *Latin* At first sight, first impression.

primely Excellently.

privative Depriving.

privity *Law* The relation between privies.

prize *British* To pry something open.

pro *Latin* In front of, for, on behalf of, on account of.

proa A sailing boat with a single outrigger.

Probate, Divorce & Admiralty
British A court handling
wills, wives and wrecks.
probative Evidential.
probity Integrity, honesty.
proboscis An elephant's trunk.
proces-verbal *French* Written
report of proceedings.
prochein *Law* Nearest.
procumbent Lying on the face.
procurer A pimp.
proem Preface or preamble.
profert *Law* An exhibition of
a document in court.
profluent Flowing smoothly.
prog *Slang* Search or prowl
for plunder or food.
prognosticate To forecast,
predict or prophesy.
projet *French* A draft of a
proposed document.
prolate Elongated along the
polar diameter.
prolegomenon A preliminary
observation.
prolepsis Anticipation.
prolonge *French* A rope with
a hook at one end and a
toggle at the other.
prolusion A preliminary essay,
article or attempt.
pro memoria *Latin* For memory
(used to recall rights).
promiscuous Of mixed and
disorderly composition.
promulgate To make known to
the public, publish.

proneur *French* Eulogist.

pronunciamento *Spanish* Proclamation, manifesto.

proof spirit One containing fifty percent alcohol.

propaedeutic Of preliminary instruction.

prophylactic Protecting from disease.

propinquity Proximity.

propitious Favorable.

propolis Red resin got by bees from buds and used to stop up crevices.

propriety Conformity to established standards.

pro re nata *Latin* For an unexpected contingency.

prorogue To discontinue a session.

proscenium *Theater* The part of the stage in front of the curtain.

proscribe Denounce, condemn, prohibit, banish.

prosector One who dissects dead bodies and prepares them for lectures.

proselyte Convert from one opinion to another.

proser One who talks or writes prosaically.

prosit *Latin* (as a toast) May it do good.

prosopopoeia The introduction of a pretended speaker or personification of an abstract thing.

prosthodontia The replacement of missing teeth.

protean Variable, versatile.

pro tem *Latin* For the time being, temporarily.

protium Ordinary hydrogen, as opposed to heavy hydrogen.

provenance *French* The place of origin.

provender Fodder, hay.

prurient Given to indulgence of lewd ideas.

prussic acid Hydrocyanic acid.

pseudograph A spurious literary work.

pseudologer A systematic liar.

psi Pounds per square inch.

psittacine Like a parrot.

psychosomatic Caused by an emotional state.

psychrometer A wet and dry bulb thermometer.

ptisan A nourishing concoction.

pub *British* A tavern (short for public house).

publican *British* The keeper of a public house.

pudency Modesty.

pug Loam or clay mixed with water for brickmaking.

puisne *Law* Younger, inferior in rank, junior.

pukka *Indian* Reliable, good.

pule To cry in a thin voice, whine, whimper.

pullet A young hen.

pulverulent Powdery, of dust.

punctilio A fine point of ceremony or proceedure.

pundit A Hindu scholar or learned man.

pung A sleigh with a boxlike body on runners.

punty An iron rod, used to handle molten glass.

purblind Nearly blind.

purdah *Indian* Screen hiding women from strangers.

purl (of a brook) To flow with a whirling motion and a babbling sound.

purser A ship's officer who keeps the accounts.

pursy Short winded, puffy, corpulent.

purvey *British* To provide, furnish or supply.

purview Range of operation, activity, concern.

pusillanimous Faint-hearted, mean-spirited.

putative Reputed, supposed.

putlog Horizontal timber to support scaffolding.

putsch *German* A minor revolt or uprising.

puttee Long strip of cloth wound around a leg from the ankle to the knee.

puttier One who putties.

pwt Pennyweight.

pyretic Of fever.

pyriform Pear shaped.

pyromancy Divination by fire
    or forms seen in it.
Pyrrhic victory One gained
    at too great a cost.
python A posessing spirit.
pythonic Prophetic, oracular.
pyxis Small box, casket.

Q

Q.E.D. Quod erat demon-
    strandum *Latin* That
    has been proved.
Q.P. Quantum placet *Latin*
    As much as you like.
quadrate Square, rectangular.
quadricycle A vehicle like a
    tricycle with 4 wheels.
quadrillion 1 followed by 15
    zeros (24 in Britain).
quadrival Having four roads
    meeting at a point.
quaere *Latin* I should like
    to know.
quagmire A quaking bog.
quand meme *French* Just the
    same.
quant *British* A punting pole
    with a flange at the end.
quarry A small pane of glass
    used in windows.
quarterdeck The upper deck of
    a ship from the mainmast
    to the stern.

quarter section A piece of
 land half a mile square.
quarto A book size about nine
 and a half by 12 inches.
quash Annul, make void, put
 an end to.
quasi *Latin* As if, as it
 were, resembling.
quass *Russian* Beer made of
 barley, malt and rye.
quean An impudent or badly be-
 haved girl, jade, hussy.
Queen Mab *Irish* A fairy who
 governs the dreams of men.
quercine Of oak.
querist One who puts a query.
querulous Complaining, peevish.
queue *British* A line of people
 waiting for something.
quicklime Unslaked lime.
quid *British* A pound sterling.
quiddity Essence of a thing.
quidnunc *Latin* What now? (a
 person given to gossip).
quid pro quo *Latin* One thing
 in return for another.
quien sabe *Spanish* Who knows?
quiescent Motionless, inert,
 silent, dormant.
quietude Tranquility, calm-
 ness, stillness.
quietus Anything that ends or
 settles a matter.
quinary Of the number five.
quintal 100 kilograms.
quintessence The purest form
 of a quality or class.

quintillion 1 followed by 18
zeros (30 in Britain).
quire 24 sheets of paper.
quirt A short riding whip.
quitclaim *Law* A transfer of
all one's interest.
qui tam *Law* (action brought
by) An informer.
quittance Recompense.
qui va la *French* Who goes
there?
quiver A case to hold arrows.
qui vive *French* (on the)
Alert, waiting for some-
thing to happen.
quoad hoc *Latin* In this
respect, to this extent.
quoin An external angle of a
wall or building.
quondam That formerly was.
quotidian Daily, everyday.

R

rabbet A cut in the edge of a
board, to fit another.
rabbitry A collection of
rabbits.
rabid Irrationally extreme,
violent, unreasoning.
raceway *British* A passage
for water, millrace.
rach Wreck, destruction.
raconteur *French* A story
teller.

radar Radio direction and range finding equipment.

raddle Interweave, wattle.

radian 57.2958 degrees.

raff The riffraff, rabble.

raffle *Nautical* A tangle (of rope or canvas).

rag *British* To tease, play practical jokes on.

ragtag and bobtail The riffraff.

rail Use abusive language.

raillery Good humored ridicule, banter.

raison d'etre *French* The reason for a thing's existence.

raj *India* Rule, dominion.

rake The slope of the stage in a theater.

rallentando *Music* Becoming slower.

R.A.M. *Airline* The Raggedy Assed Masses (see E.I.P., V.I.P. & U.L.P.).

ramiform Like a branch.

rand A strip of leather in a shoe for leveling.

randy *British* Lustful.

rank Growing too luxuriantly.

rape Refuse of grapes, used as filter in making vinegar.

rapine Plundering.

rappee A coarse kind of snuff.

rapport *French* Relation.

rapprochment *French* Reestablishment of an harmonious

relationship.

rapscallion Rascal, rogue.

raptorial Predatory.

rara avis *Latin* A rare thing
or person (rare bird).

raree show A peep show.

rasorial Given to scratching
the ground for food.

rat *Slang* To betray.

ratal *British* The amount on
which rates are assessed.

rate To scold.

rathskeller *German* The cellar
of a town hall, often used
as a beer hall.

ratiocination Reasoning.

rationale Statement of reasons.

ratlines Lines across a ship's
shrouds as ladder rungs.

rattus rattus The common
brown rat.

ravelment Entanglement.

raven To go plundering, eat
voraciously.

rayah Any subject of the
Sultan of Turkey who is
not a Mohammedan.

razee Ship reduced in height by
removal of upper decks.

R.C. Right center (of a stage).

re *Latin* In the matter of.

realgar An orange-red mineral
used in pyrotechnics.

Realpolitik *German* Policy
based on power, rather
than ideals.

real wages Wages estimated in

their purchasing power.

ream 500 sheets (of paper).

rebeldom A region controlled by rebels.

reboant Bellowing in return.

rebus Representation of name or word, by pictures that suggest its syllables.

rebutter *Law* A defendant's answer to a plaintiff's surrejoinder.

recalesce To get hot again.

recede To give back to a previous owner.

recension Revision of text.

rechauffé *French* A warmed up dish, a rehash.

recherche *French* Sought out with care.

recidivism Relapse into crime.

recipe *Latin* Take (thou).

reciprocal ohm A mho.

recision Invalidation.

reclame *French* Publicity.

recondite Abstruse, little known.

recourse Going to a possible source of help.

recreant Cowardly, craven.

recrudesce To break out again.

rectilinear In or forming a straight line.

recto *Printing* The right hand page of an open book.

recurve To curve back.

recusant Refusing to submit or comply.

recuse *Law* To challenge a
    judge or juror as being
    disqualified to act.
redact To put into literary
    form, revise, edit.
redbait To denounce as a
    political radical.
redd To put in order, tidy.
redirect *Law* Examination of
    a witness by the party
    calling him, after cross
    examination.
redolent Reminiscent.
redoubtable Formidable.
redound To have an effect.
reductio ad absurdum *Latin*
    Reduction to absurdity.
    (to refute a proposition).
reef *Nautical* To reduce the
    area of a sail.
reefer A marijuana cigarette.
refectory A dining hall in
    an institution.
reflecting telescope One with
    a mirror, rather than a
    lens, for the main image.
reflet *French* Luster, irid-
    escence (on pottery).
refluent Flowing back.
refractory Stubborn, unman-
    ageable, rebellious.
refulgent Shining, radiant,
    glowing.
regelate To freeze together.
registrar A recorder (of docu-
    ments, facts, etc.).
regrate To buy goods to sell

again at a profit.

reify Convert into a concrete thing, materialize.

rejectamenta *Latin* Refuse, waste mater, things cast up by the sea.

rejoin To say in answer.

rejoinder An answer to a reply, a retort.

relume Rekindle, light again, make bright again.

R.E.M. Rapid eye movement (that occurs in light sleep).

remarque *French* A mark indicating a stage in the engraving of a plate.

remise *Law* Surrender, make over (right, property).

renal Of the kidneys.

renege Go back on one's word.

renitent Resisting pressure, recalcitrant.

rentier *French* Person who does not need to earn a living.

rent-seck Rental in which there is no right to collect by seizing the tenant's goods.

repaint A repainted golf ball.

repellant Repulsive.

repine Fret, be discontented.

replevin *Law* Recovery of goods taken pending court action.

replication Reply to an answer.

reposit To put back, replace.

repoussé *French* (of metal work) Hammered into relief from the reverse side.

reprieve Suspend or delay execution of condemned man.

reprise *Law* An annual charge taken from an estate.

reprobate An unprincipled, abandoned person (beyond hope of salvation).

reptant *Zoology* Creeping.

republic of letters The body of literary people.

res *Latin* Thing.

rescind Revoke, annul.

rescission Rescinding.

reseau A network.

res gestae *Latin* Achievements.

resile Recoil, rebound, resume previous shape and size.

res judicata *Latin* A case that has been decided.

resorb To absorb again.

respirator *British* Gas mask.

res publica *Latin* The state.

restive Unmanageable.

resusticate To revive.

retenue *French* Reserve, self control.

reticular Like a net.

reticule A small purse or bag.

retorsion Retaliation by the same act as another state (as high tariffs).

retrocede To go back, recede.

retrorse Turned backward.

retroussé *French* Turned up (of a nose).

reveille *French* A bugle call for soldiers to wake up.

revenant *French* One returned
from the dead, or exile.
revers *French* Part of a garment turned back, to show
the lining or facing.
revetment A facing of masonry
protecting an embankment.
revivify Restore to animation,
activity, vigor, or life.
rhabdomancy Use of a divining
rod (as to find water).
Rhadamanthus A stern and
incorruptible judge.
rheoscope An instrument that
indicates the presence of
an electric current.
rheotropisn The effect of a
current of water on the
direction of plant growth.
rhetor A master of rhetoric.
rhigolene A volatile liquid
used to produce local
anesthesia by freezing.
rhinal Of the nose.
rhumbatron Cavity resonator.
rhumb line That followed by a
ship sailing continuously
on the same course.
rialto An exchange or mart.
riant Smiling, cheerful.
rich rhyme Syllables having
the same sound but quite
different meanings.
rick *British* A stack of hay
or straw (often thatched).
rickey Gin, lime juice and
carbonated water.

rident Laughing, smiling.

rifacimento *Italian* A remod-
elled form of a literary
or musical work.

riffle *Mining* A groove in a
trough or sluice to catch
particles of gold.

right ho *British* Yes, okay.

rigor mortis *Latin* Stiffen-
ing of a body after death.

Rig-Veda *Hinduism* The oldest
sacred document, among the
world's living religions.

rill A rivulet or brook.

rimose Full of chinks or
fissures.

ringent Gaping, grinning.

rip An area of broken water
at sea or in a river.

R.I.P. Requiescat in pace *Latin*
May he rest in peace.

riparian Of a river bank.

rip cord One that causes a
a parachute to open.

riposte Counterstroke, retort.

ripping *British* Splendid!

riprap Stones used to protect
sea walls, et cetera.

risible Inclined to laugh.

ritardando *Music* Becoming
gradually slower.

rive To tear or rend apart.

river horse A hippopotamus.

riverine Of a river.

riviere *French* A necklace
of gems, usually with
more than one string.

road agent A highwayman.

road metal Small stones used to make roads.

road runner A terrestial cuckoo of America.

roband *Nautical* A piece of spun yarn used to secure a sail to a yard.

roborant Strengthening.

roche moutonnee *French* A knob of rock, rounded and smoothed by glacial action.

rollick To be jovial, enjoy life boisterously.

roman a clef *French* A novel in which real people and events are disguised as fiction.

rooftree Ridgepole of a roof.

roorback A false report put out for political effect.

ropewalk A long, covered place where ropes are made.

ropy Inferior, shabby.

rose cold Hay fever caused by the pollen of roses.

rostrate Having a rostrum.

roturier *French* Plebeian.

roué *French* Debauchee, rake (deserving to be broken on the wheel).

rouleau *Music* A florid solo vocal passage

roundhouse *Railroad* A place for locomotives, built around a turntable.

round robin A petition with the signatures in a circle

to hide their order.

roustabout A wharf laborer or
     deckhand (on a river).

roux *French* Mixture of fat &
     flour to thicken sauces.

rover *Archery* A mark select-
     ed at random.

rowel Spiked revolving disk
     at the end of a spur.

rowen The second crop of grass
     or hay in a season.

rowlock *British* Oarlock.

royal flush *Poker* The five
     highest cards of one suit.

rpm Revolutions per minute.

RSVP Respondez s'il vous plait
     French Please reply.

rubric A title or heading in
     a book written in red (or
     in special lettering).

ruck Main body of competitors
     left out of the running.

rue Regret, repent of.

ruff *Cards* Trumping when one
     can not follow suit.

ruffle Low beating on a drum,
     less loud than a roll.

ruga A wrinkle, fold or ridge.

rugger *British* Rugby football.

rum *British* Odd, strange.

rundle A rung of a ladder.

run-in *Printing* Matter that
     is added to a text.

run-through *Theater* Rehearsal.

rusticate Go to the country.

rye *Gypsy* A gentleman.

Rx Recipe *Latin* Take (thou).

S

sabot *French* A shoe made from
a single piece of wood.
sabulous Sandy, gritty.
saccharin A compound 400 times
as sweet as sugar.
saccharize Convert into sugar.
sacerdotal Of priests.
sachem *American Indian* Chief.
sackless *Scottish* Dispirited,
without energy.
sacral Of religious rites.
saddletree Frame of a saddle.
sadiron A solid flatiron.
sahib *Indian* Master, friend.
said *Law* Mentioned before.
Saint Agnes' Eve Jan 20, when
rites are held to reveal
a woman's future husband.
salacious Lustful, lecherous.
salad days Days of youthful
inexperience.
salient Prominent, conspicuous.
saliferous Containing salt.
salle a manger *French* Dining
room.
saltant Dancing, leaping.
saltern A place to evaporate
sea water, to get salt.
salubrious Healthy.
salve *Latin* Be in good health!
salver A tray.
samovar *Russian* An urn to boil
water to make tea.

sanative Healing.
sanbenito A yellow garment worn by a condemned heretic at a Spanish Inquisition.
sandglass An hourglass.
sandwich man A man with advertizing boards hung from his shoulders, front & back.
sanguinary Bloody.
sanguine Hopeful, cheerful.
sans *French* Without.
Sansei A grandchild of Japanese immigrants to the USA.
sans pareil *French* Without equal.
sans souci *French* Carefree.
sapid Having flavor.
sapiental Of wisdom.
saponaceous Soapy.
sapphism Lesbianism.
sartorial Of a tailor.
sahay To glide or move.
satiate To supply to excess, so as to disgust or weary.
saturnine Of sluggish, gloomy temperament.
saturnism Lead poisoning.
sauerkraut *German* Cabbage cut finely, salted and allowed to ferment until sour.
sauve qui peut *French* Let he who can save himself (in a rout or stampede).
savanna A grassy plain with scattered trees.
savant A man of learning.
savate French boxing, with feet

and head as well as fists.

saveloy *British* A highly seas-
oned, dried sausage.

savoir vivre *French* Knowledge
of the world and the usages
of polite society.

saw log One large enough to be
sawn into boards.

saxatile Living among rocks.

sbirro *Italian* A policeman.

scab A workman who refuses to
help his trade union.

scabble To dress stone roughly.

scabland Rough, barren, land
with little vegatation.

scagliola Plasterwork imitat-
ing marble, granite, etc.

scalage A deduction allowed in
dealing with goods likely
to shrink, leak or other-
wise vary in weight.

scallion An onion that does
not have a large bulb.

scandent Climbing (as a plant).

SCAPA *British* The Society
for Checking the Abuses of
Public Advertising.

scar *British* A precipitous
rocky place, a cliff.

scarcement A ledge formed by a
setback in a wall.

scarehead A newspaper headline
in large type.

scarfskin The outer layer of
skin, the epidermis.

scarify To lacerate by severe
criticism.

Scarlet letter A red letter
'A' worn by people convic-
ted of adultery.

scarp A steep slope.

schema A synopsis, outline,
diagram or plan.

scherzando *Music* Playful.

schmo A foolish, boring or
stupid person, a jerk.

schnorrer *Yiddish* A beggar.

schooner A very tall glass
(as for beer).

sciamachy Fighting with
a shadow, or with an
imaginary enemy.

sciential Having knowledge.

scilicet Namely, to wit.

scintilla A spark, a minute
particle, a trace.

sciolist A superficial preten-
der to knowledge.

sciolto *Music* In free manner.

scion A descendant.

scissile Able to be cut.

sclaff *Golf* To scrape the
ground with a club before
hitting the ball.

sclerous Hard, firm, bony.

sconce To fine.

score About 20 pounds, used in
weighing pigs or oxen.

scoria The slag left after
smelting metals.

scour Rove, range, go hastily
in search or pursuit.

scouse *Nautical* A baked food
served to sailors.

scout To reject with scorn
     or ridicule.
scrimshaw Accomplish a small
     mechanical task neatly.
scroop Make a grating noise.
scrouge To squeeze, crowd.
scrunch To crunch, crush.
scrutator An investigator.
scuff To walk without raising
     the feet, shuffle.
sculpsit *Latin* He (or she)
     engraved or carved it.
scumble Soften a painting by a
     thin coat of opaque color.
scupper Hole in ship's side to
     carry off water from deck.
scurrilous Grossly abusive.
scut A short tail.
scuttlebutt *Nautical* Gossip,
     rumor.
sea calf The harbor seal.
sea hog A porpoise.
sea lawyer An argumentative
     or querulous sailor.
sealed book Something past
     understanding.
seashore *Law* The land between
     high and low water marks.
seawan Beads made from sea
     shells, once used by
     native Americans as money.
sec *French* Dry, not sweet.
second growth That which fol-
     lows the destruction of
     virgin forest.
secondo *Music* The second part
     in a duet.

sectile Able to be cut.

secundum *Latin* According to.

se defendendo *Law* Defending himself (a plea used in a homicide trial).

sedulous Diligent, persevering.

segno *Music* A sign or mark (at the beginning or end of a repetition).

seiche Lateral oscillation of water in a lake.

seine A vertical fishing net with floats at the top and weights at the bottom.

seised *Law* Having posession of a freehold estate.

seism An earthquake.

semiotic Of signs or symptoms.

sempre *Music* Throughout.

sententious Aphoristic, pithy, affectedly judical.

sentient Having the power of perception by the senses.

seq Sequens *Latin* The following (one).

serac A large block of ice on a glacier.

seraglio The part of a Mohammedan house where wives and concubines are secluded.

serai A caravansery (a lodging place for caravans).

serein Very fine rain, from a clear sky, after sunset.

serendipity The faculty of making happy, unexpected discoveries by accident.

seriatim Point by point, in a series, one after another.
sericulture Keeping silkworms.
serry Crowd closely together.
setaceous Bristly.
set chisel One for shearing off nails or rivets.
severalty Individual, unshared tenure of estate, etc.
sextillion 1 followed by 21 zeros (36 in Britain).
sforzando *Music* With sudden emphasis.
s.g. Specific gravity.
shadoof Long pole with bucket and counterweight, used in Egypt to raise water.
shah King.
shakedown A makeshift bed.
shaman A medecine man.
shammy Chamois.
shandy *British* A mixture of beer and ginger beer.
shanghai To drug a man and ship him as a sailor.
Shangrila A secret airfield.
sharper A shrewd swindler.
sharp-set Very hungry.
shavetail Second lieutenant.
Shavian (in the manner) of George Bernard Shaw.
shebang *Slang* Thing, affair.
shellback An old sailor.
Sheol Hebrew Hades.
shikar *Hindu* Hunting.
shill Accomplice of a street peddlar, gambler, etc.

shillelagh An Irish cudgel of blackthorn or oak.

shingle *British* Small rounded stones on seashore.

shinplaster Paper money of little value.

ship chandler *British* Dealer in cordage, canvas and other supplies for ships.

shipway A structure that supports a ship being built.

shivaree A mock serenade with kettles, horns, etc.

short-commons A scanty allowance of food.

short shrift Short time given a condeemned man for confession, before execution.

short ton 2,000 pounds.

shot Woven to show a play of colors (as silk).

S.H.P. Shaft horsepower.

shyster A dishonest lawyer.

sibilant Hissing.

sibyl A pagan prophetess.

sic *Latin* Thus (used to say a thing was copied exactly).

sic (to a dog) Attack.

sic passim *Latin* The same wherever found.

side light Incidental information.

siderial Determined by the stars.

sierra *Spanish* Long, jagged mountain chain.

sight draft One payable on

presentation.
sightly With a fine view.
sigli *Latin* A seal.
signalize To make notable.
signalment A description of a
 person (for the police).
signature A number of sheets of
 paper folded so as to form
 a section of a book.
silica gel A highly absorbent
 gelatinous form of silica.
silviculture Forestry.
s'll vous plait *French* Please.
simian Of a monkey.
simon-pure Real, genuine.
simony Making profit out of
 sacred things.
simp *Slang* A fool.
simplex Simple.
simulacrum A mere, faint or
 unreal semblance.
sine *Latin* Without.
sine die *Latin* Without a date
 for future action.
sine qua non *Latin* Something
 essential, indispensable.
sinfonia *Music* A symphony.
single-foot A gait of a horse.
singlet *British* A kind of
 undershirt worn by men.
Sinicism Chinese customs.
sinistral On the left side.
sinistrous Unlucky, disastrous.
sinking fund A fund to pay
 off a debt.
sinuous With many curves,
 indirect, devious.

sipid Having a pleasing taste
    or flavor.
sire The male parent of
    a quadruped.
sirocco The hot, dry wind of
    Africa reaching Europe.
sitomania An insane craving
    for food.
sitophobia An insane aversion
    to food.
situs *Latin* Position.
sixty fourth note *Music* A
    hemidemisemiquaver.
skedaddle *Slang* To run away.
skeleton key One filed down to
    open various locks.
skiff A boat small enough
    to be rowed, or sailed,
    by one person.
skipknot One easily undone.
skirr To go rapidly, fly.
skoal *Swedish* Health! (as
    a toast).
sleeping partner *British* A
    silent partner.
sleight Dexterity, skill.
slew A marshy pool or inlet.
slop shop Cheap clothing shop.
slots Devices along the leading
    edges of airplane wings to
    increase lift at low speed.
slowworm A blindworm.
sloyd *Swedish* A system of
    manual training in wood-
    working, etc.
small beer *British* People or
    things of no importance.

smart money *Law* Punitive or exemplary damages.

smolt A young salmon.

S.M.P. Sine mascula prole *Latin* Without male issue.

snaffle *British* Appropriate, purloin, pinch.

SNAFU Situation Normal, All Fouled Up.

snaggletooth A tooth growing apart from the others.

snapping turtle A large and savage turtle.

snath The shaft or handle of a scythe.

snell A piece of gut between a fish hook and a line.

snib A bolt or catch to fasten a door or window.

snifter A very small drink of liquor.

sniggle To fish for eels by pushing a baited hook into their hole.

snitch *Slang* An informer.

snood A short line between a hook and the main line (in fishing at sea).

snoot *Slang* Nose.

snowbird A cocaine addict.

snow line A line above which there is always snow.

sobriquet *French* A nickname.

societal Of social groups.

sockdolager Something very large, heavy or decisive.

sodality An association or

fraternity.

soft pedal *British* To tone down, make less strong.

softwood Coniferous.

softy One who is easily imposed upon.

soi-disant *French* Self styled, pretended.

solecism An error in grammar, idiom or behaviour.

solstice When the sun is farthest from the equator.

solus *Theater* Alone.

solute The substance dissolved in a given solution.

somnabulism Sleep walking.

somniloquy Talking in one's sleep.

sonant Sounding.

sonatina *Music* A short or simplified sonata.

soniferous Conveying or producing sound.

sophism A false argument intended to deceive.

sordamente *Music* In a muffled manner.

sororate Marriage with a wife's sister.

sortilege Divination by lots.

S.O.S. Signal of distress used in Morse code.

sot A confirmed drunkard.

sotto voce *Italian* In an undertone, aside.

soubrette *Theater* A pert maid servant.

sounding Measuring the depth
(of water, etc.).

soupcon *French* A suspicion,
a very small amount.

sousaphone A bass tuba.

southeaster *Nautical* A
storm from the southeast.

southpaw *Slang* Left handed.

sou'wester *Nautical* A wide-
brimmed, waterproof hat.

soviet *Russian* A council.

S.P. *Betting* Starting price.

spall A splinter or chip.

span A pair of horses, etc.
harnessed together.

Spanish Main The northeast
coast of South America.

spanking Striking, notable.

sparable A small, headless nail
used by shoemakers.

sparge To scatter or sprinkle.

spate *British* A river-flood.

spear side The male side of
a family.

special partner One whose lia-
bility for a firm's debts is
limited to his investment.

specie Coin, coined money.

specious Plausible, apparently
right but deceptive.

specular Like a mirror.

speculum *Latin* A mirror
or reflector.

spelean Of caves.

selter Zinc in ingots.

spelunker One who explores caves.

sphenic Wedge shaped.

spheroid Almost like a sphere.

spile A wooden peg, spigot.

spill A thin piece of wood to light candles, etc.

spinet A small harpsichord.

spinney *British* A small wood, a thicket.

spirituel *French* (of women) Refined, graceful.

spirket *Nautical* A space between the floor timbers.

spiroid Like a spiral.

spitoon A cuspidor.

splat A broad, flat piece of wood.

spoof *British* Hoax, humbug.

sporran *Scottish* A purse.

sprag A block to check a wheel of a vehicle.

spring tides Those having the most rise and fall.

sprue An opening through which metal is poured into a mold.

spud A small spade to cut the roots of weeds, etc.

spurrier A maker of spurs.

sq Square.

squared ring A boxing ring.

squiffy *British* Slightly drunk.

stack To make airplanes wait at various levels, before being allowed to land.

staff Plaster for temporary ornamental buildings.

stager An old hand, an experienced person.

staging post A regular stopping

place on an air route.

stalactite Deposit hanging from the roof of a cave.

stalagmite Deposit sticking up from the floor of a cave

stalking horse *Politics* Candidate used to draw votes away from a rival.

stannary A tin mining place.

starboard The right side of a ship, facing forward (early ships had external rudders on that side).

status quo *Latin* The state in which a thing was or is.

statutable Legally punishable.

steatopygia Abnormal accumulation of fat on buttocks.

steelyard A portable balance.

steeve To pack tightly.

stein *German* A beer mug.

steppe A large, treeless plain.

stere *French* A cubic meter.

sterling Genuine, of standard value or purity.

sternway Backward movement (of a ship).

stertorous Of heavy snoring.

stevedore A man who loads and unloads ships.

steward One who manages others' property or finances.

sthenic Sturdy, heavily built.

stiacciato *Art* In very low relief.

stickful *Printing* All the type a composing stick will hold.

still hunt A quiet or secret pursuit of anything.

stilliform Drop shaped.

stipend Fixed, regular pay.

stipple Paint or draw in dots.

stirps A stock, a family.

stirrup cup *British* A farewell drink.

stithy An anvil.

stoat The ermine (when brown).

stomatic Of the mouth.

stone *British* 14 pounds (used to weigh people and fish).

stonewall *Cricket* Excessively cautious batting.

stony broke *British* Having no money at all.

stooge An entertainer who feeds lines to a comedian.

stool pigeon A secret confederate, decoy or spy.

stope *Mining* An excavation to remove accessible ore.

stop order An order to a broker to sell stock if the market reaches a certain price.

stopple A stopper, for a bottle or other vessel.

strafe To attack with machine gun fire from airplanes.

straight flush *Poker* 5 successive cards of the same suit.

strand line A shore line.

strepitous Noisy.

stridor A harsh, grating or creaking sound.

struthious Like an ostrich.

St. Swithin's Day July 15th.
stub nail A short, thick nail.
stull *Mining* A timber prop.
stultify *Law* To allege or
    prove to be insane.
stunner *British* A girl of
    striking beauty.
sty *British* A pig pen.
subacute Somewhat acute.
subaqueous Under water.
subaudition Understanding of
    what is not expressed.
subcutaneous Under the skin.
subereous Like cork.
subito *Music* Suddenly.
subjacent Underlying, below.
subjective Existing in the
    mind (not objective).
sub judice *Latin* Before
    the judge.
suborn Induce (by bribery)
    to commit perjury.
subpoena A writ commanding
    a person's attendance
    in a court of justice.
subrogation *Law* Substitu-
    tion of one party for
    another as creditor.
sub rosa *Latin* Privately,
    confidentially.
subscript Written below.
substructure A foundation.
subsume To include under
    a rule or class.
succedaneum A substitute, a
    thing to fall back on.
succes d'estime *French* A

cordial reception given
to a work from respect.

succuba A female demon who
has sexual intercourse
with sleeping men.

sudatory Causing sweating.

sudor Sweat, perspiration.

sufferance Tolerance.

suffrage The right to vote.

suffuse To overspread with a
liquid, color, etc.

sui generis *Latin* Unique,
of its own kind.

sui juris *Law* One able to be
responsible for his acts.

suint The natural grease of
the wool of sheep.

suitor *Law* A plaintiff.

sultana A wife or a concubine
of a sultan.

summa cum laude *Latin* With the
highest honor or praise.

summer time *British* Daylight
saving time.

summum bonum *Latin* The
highest good.

sumptuary Regulating expend-
iture.

sumptuary law One regulating
personal habits which of-
fend the community.

sunbow A bow like a rainbow
seen in spray, etc.

sundog A small rainbow.

suo jure *Latin* In his (her
or its) own right.

suo loco *Latin* In its

rightful place.

sup Supra *Latin* Above.

supercargo A ship's officer in charge of cargo.

supercool To cool a liquid below its freezing point without it solidifying.

supererogate To do more than duty requires.

superficies The surface or outside of a thing.

superfuse To pour (a liquid) over something.

superglacial On the surface of a glacier.

superincumbent Resting on something else.

supernal Heavenly, divine.

supernatant Floating above, or on the surface.

supernumary Extra, additional.

superscript Written above.

supersedeas *Law* A writ to stay proceedings.

supertanker One with capacity of over 75,000 tons.

supine Lying face upward.

suppletory Supplying a deficiency.

supposititious Fraudulently substituted or pretended.

suppurate Form pus, fester.

surd *Mathematics* (quantity) not able to be expressed in rational numbers.

surety Pledge, guarantee.

surrogate A deputy.

suspension points Dots where
    words were deleted.
sus per coll Suspendatur per
    collum *Latin* Let him
    be hanged.
susurrant Softly murmuring,
    whispering.
sutler A camp follower who
    sells provisions, etc.
suttee A Hindu widow who im-
    molates herself on her
    husband's funeral pyre.
suum cuique *Latin* To each
    what belongs to him.
SWAG *Pentagon* A Scientific
    Wild Assed Guess.
swale A low place in a
    tract of land.
swanherd One who tends swans.
swan song A person's last
    achievement.
swarf Chips or filings of
    wood, metal, etc.
swatch A sample of cloth.
swath The space covered by
    stroke of a scythe.
sweated Underpaid and
    overworked.
sweet shop *British* A candy
    store.
swingeing Very forcible.
swing shift From about 3 PM
    until midnight.
swipe *Slang* To steal.
switchman A man in charge of
    switches on a railroad.
swot *British* To study hard.

sybarite An effeminate
voluptuary.
sycophant Flatterer, toady.
syllogism *Logic* An argument
with two premises and a
conclusion.
sylvan Of the woods.
synchronism Coincidence in
time.
syndetic Uniting, connecting.
syne *Scottish* Since.
synergy Combined action.
syntonize To tune to the
same frequency.
syzygy *Astronomy* Conjunction
or opposition.

T

T *Betting* Taken.
Taal South African Dutch.
tableau *French* A picture.
taboret A low seat without
back or arms.
tabula rasa *Latin* A mind as
yet free of impressions.
tacet *Music* Silent.
taction Touch, contact.
taffrall The rail across the
stern of a ship.
tagger Thin sheet iron.
tall *Law* Limitation of an
estate to a person.
tailrace The race leading

away from a water wheel.

tain Tin foil for the backs
of mirrors.

tales *Law* Jurors called when
there are not enough.

talion Retaliation as author-
ized by law.

talipes A clubfoot.

tallboy *British* A highboy.

talus A sloping mass of rocky
fragments at the base of
a cliff.

tant pis *French* So much the
worse (or my aunt is in
the bathroom).

tarantism An uncontrollable urge
to dance, by people who
think they have been bitten
by tarantulas.

tardo *Music* Slow.

tare Allowance for the weight
of a box or other container
in which goods are packed.

Tarheel A native of North
Carolina.

tarn *British* A small mountain
lake or pool.

tartan A single masted vessel
with a lateen sail and a jib
used in the Mediterranean.

tasimeter An electrical device
to determine minute changes
in temperature.

taurine Like a bull.

teamster A truck driver.

tea shop *British* A lunchroom.

tectonic Of construction.

ted Turn over and spread out.
tegular Of or like tiles.
telekinesis Movement at a dist-
    ance, without material con-
    nection with the agent.
teleology The doctrine of final
    causes or purposes.
tellurian Of the earth.
temblor An earthquake.
templet A pattern or gauge.
tempus fugit *Latin* Time flies.
tenantry Tenants.
tendance Attention, care.
tendentious Having an under-
    lying purpose or bias.
tenebrous Dark, gloomy.
tenon End of a piece of wood
    fashioned to fit into
    a corresponding cavity.
tensive Stretching, straining.
tenuous Thin, slender, small.
teredo A shipworm.
ternary Threefold, triple.
terpsichorean Of dancing.
terra incognita *Latin* An un-
    known or unexplored land.
terrazzo *Italian* A floor mat-
    erial of broken stone and
    cement, polished in place.
terrene Earthly, worldly.
terret A ring on a saddle for
    reins to pass through.
testamentary Of a will.
tetchy Irritable, touchy.
tete-a-tete *French* Together
    in private.
tetrad A group of four.

thaumatology The study or description of miracles.

thé dansant *French* A tea party with dancing.

the fish on five *Restaurant* The person eating fish at table number five.

theine Caffein found in tea.

thermal Of heat.

thermoplastic Soft when heated but otherwise unchanged.

thermosetting (plastic) That becomes hard when heated, and then stays hard.

theroid Having beast-like propensities.

thesaurus A store of knowledge, dictionary, encylopedia.

thesis A proposition.

Thespian An actor or actress.

thetic Positive, dogmatic.

thewless Without mental or moral vigor.

thill Shaft of cart or carriage.

thimblerig Shell game.

third estate The common people.

thole Pin in gunwale of boat to act as fulcrum for an oar.

thorough bass *Music* A bass part written out in full.

thoroughpaced (of a horse) Trained to go through all the possible paces.

thrall One who is in bondage.

thrasonical Bragging.

thunderstick A bullroarer.

tick *British* Credit.

ticket of leave *British* Parole
for a convict.
tiene duende *Spanish* There is
something magical about him.
tiffin *British* Lunch.
tigon The offspring of a tiger
and a lioness.
tilde Mark (~) put over Spanish
n when it is pronounced ny.
tiller *Nautical* Lever on head
of a rudder, for steering.
tilt A canvas cover for a cart.
timbal A kettledrum.
time immemorial *Law* Before the
year 1189 A.D.
timeserver One who adapts his
conduct to conditions.
timpani Kettledrums.
tinctorial Of coloring.
tine A sharp point or prong (as
of a fork).
tinge Color slightly.
tinker *British* A mender of pots
and pans (often ininerant).
tintinabulation The ringing or
sound of bells.
tipple A device that turns over
a freight car to empty it.
tirailleur *French* Sharpshooter.
titular Of a title.
toad spittle Cuckoo-spit.
tocsin An alarm signal sounded
on a bell or bells.
toenail *Carpentry* A nail
driven obliquely.
togated Peaceful
toile *French* Transparent linen.

tong A Chinese society.

tonsorial Of a barber.

tontine Annuity shared by sub-
scribers to a loan.

top banana The senior comedian
in a vaudeville show.

top dress To manure (land) on
the surface.

tophamper Unnecessary weight.

top hole *British* First rate!

topi *India* A pith sun helmet.

topiary Art of clipping shrubs
into ornamental shapes.

top kick A first sergeant.

toplofty Haughty, pretentious.

topography Detailed description
of a limited area.

toponym A place name.

topping *British* Excellent.

top secret Extreemly secret.

tor *British* Hill, rocky peak.

toreador *Spanish* A bullfighter
who fights on horseback.

torero *Spanish* A bullfighter
who fights on foot.

tormentor *Theater* A curtain
behind the proscrenium on
each side of the stage.

torpor State of suspended physi-
cal powers & activities.

tort *Law* A civil wrong.

tortile Twisted or coiled.

tortious *Law* Of a tort.

tosh *British* Nonsense.

tot *British* A small drink.

toto caelo *Latin* By the whole
sky (an immense distance).

tot up *British* To add up.
touché *French* Good point!
tour de force *French* A feat of skill or ingenuity.
tout a fait *French* Entirely.
tout a vous *French* Yours sincerely.
tout de suite *French* At once.
tout le monde *French* Everyone.
tovarisch *Russian* Comrade.
towpath A path along a bank of a canal or river, used for towing boats.
toxic Of a poison.
tracasseries *French* Petty worries and entanglements.
trackwalker A man who inspects railroad tracks.
trading post A general store in a thinly settled region.
traditive Traditional.
traduce To slander, malign.
trailing edge The rear edge of an airfoil or propeller.
trail rope A guide rope on a balloon.
train oil Oil made of blubber from whales or seals.
tram *Machining* Correct position or adjustment.
tramcar *British* A streetcar.
trammel A thing that hinders free action, a restraint.
trammel net One designed to entangle fish.
tramway An overhead cable to carry ore or skiers.

transcalent Pervious to heat.
transcurrent Running across.
transect To cut across.
transflux A flowing across,
     through or beyond.
transfuse To pour from one
     container to another.
transhumance The seasonal
     moving of livestock from
     one region to another.
transilient Extending across
     from one point to another.
transmogrify Change by magic.
transmundane Beyond this world.
transmute To change the form,
     nature or substance of.
transpicuous Transparent.
transpontine Across a bridge.
traps Belongings, baggage.
tray agriculture Hydroponics.
treasure-trove *Law* Money of
     unknown ownership, found
     hidden in the earth.
treatise Any writing that
     deals systematically with
     a definite subject.
treenail A cylindrical piece
     of hardwood, for fastening
     timbers together.
treillage Latticework.
tremor Trembling, quivering.
trenchant Keen, incisive.
trencherman A person with a
     hearty appetite.
tret *Commerce* An allowance of
     weight for loss occurring
     in transportation.

trews Tight tartan trousers.
trey *Cards or dice* Three.
triad A group of three.
tribadism Lesbianism.
trice A moment, an instant.
trichroic Having three colors.
tricyclic Having three cycles.
trig Trim, neat, smart.
triganous Having three wives.
trigo Wheat.
trillion i followed by 12
    zeros (18 in Britain).
tripedal Having three feet.
triple crown The pope's tiara.
triptych A picture or carving
    on 3 panels, side by side.
trismus Lockjaw.
triste *French* Sad.
trivet An iron tripod to hold
    cooking vessels.
troglodyte A cave dweller.
troika *Russian* A team of three
    horses abreast.
trop *French* Too many or much.
trotline A long fishing line
    with many hooks, attached
    to it by short ones.
trounce To beat severely.
trouvaille *French* A lucky
    find, windfall.
trover *Law* Action to recover
    personal property (brought
    against the finder).
truck Vegetables, etc. grown
    for the market.
truckle Submit or yield obseq-
    uiously or tamely.

truculent Brutally harsh, savagely threatening.

trump To devise deceitfully or unfairly (as a charge).

truncheon *British* A club carried by a policeman.

trunnel A treenail.

try square *Carpentry* A device to lay out right angles.

tryst An appointed meeting.

tsunami An very large wave at sea, caused by an underwater earthquake.

tubal Of a tube.

tulle Fine silk or rayon net, used in dressmaking.

tumblebug A dung beetle.

tumbrel A dump cart.

tumid Swollen.

tumulus A mound of earth.

tun A large cask for liquids (like beer or wine).

tundra Barren arctic regions where subsoil is frozen.

tuppence *British* Two pennies.

tuque *Canadian* A knitted cap.

tu quoque *Latin* You also, or the same to you.

turbary A piece of land where turf or peat may be dug.

turbid (of liquids) Muddy, thick, not clear.

turfman One interested in horse racing.

turgid Swollen or pompous.

turned comma *Printing* An inverted comma.

turner A tumbler, gymnast.
turn key A prison keeper.
turnplate *British* A rail-
    road turntable.
turpitude Shameful depravity.
tussock *British* A clump,
    hillock, of grass etc.
tutelage Guardianship.
tutti *Music* All together.
tutu *French* A ballet skirt.
twelvemonth *British* A year.
twibill A mattock with one
    arm like that of an adz
    and one like an ax.
twice-laid Made from strands
    of used rope.
twig *British* To look at.
twit *British* A silly person.
two-by-four Unimportant.
tyke A cur.
tympanist A person who
    plays the drums, etc.
    in an orchestra.
typhoon A violent hurricane
    in the China seas.
tyro A beginner, a novice.

U

**ua mau ke ea o ka aina i ka
    pono** *Hawaiian* The life
    of the land is founded in
    righteousness.
ubiquity The capacity of being

everywhere at the same time.

ubi supra *Latin* In the place
previously referred to.

udometer A rain gauge.

U.K. United Kingdom (Britain).

ullage Loss of wine or spirit
from its container due to
leakage or evaporation.

ulotricious Having woolly hair.

U.L.P. *Airline* Unimportant Little People, including minor
film stars and the mayors
of small cities (see E.I.P.,
V.I.P. & R.A.M.).

ultima *Latin* Last, most remote.

ultima Thule The uttermost
degree attainable.

ultra vires *Latin* Beyond one's
power or authority.

ulu A knife used by Eskimos.

ululate Howl like a wolf.

umbles Edible offal of deer.

umbrageous Affording shade.

umiak An open Eskimo boat for
goods and pasengers.

unapt Unfitted, unsuited.

unbated Not bated or lessened.

unbitted Not bitted or bridled.

unbolted Not sifted (as grain).

unconscionable Unscrupulous.

undercroft A vault or chamber
beneath a church.

undershot (water wheel) driven
by water passimg beneath.

undervest *British* Undershirt.

underwhelmed *British* The opposite of overwhelmed.

underwood Underbrush.
unequivocal Clear, plain.
unguent A soft preparation or
    salve for sores, etc.
unhorse To throw from a horse.
unicameral Consisting of a
    single chamber.
unicorn A fabulous animal said
    to elude every captor save
    a virgin and seldom caught.
unkempt Not combed (as hair).
unkenned *Scottish* Unknown.
unlaid Untwisted (as a rope).
unlive To undo or annul (one's
    past life, etc).
unmeet Not fitting, unseemly.
unmentionables Trousers or
    breeches.
unrig To undress.
unsearchable Inscrutable.
unsight Without inspection
    or examination.
unswear To retract, recant.
unwitting Not knowing.
unwonted Unaccustomed, unused.
upset price The lowest price
    that a seller is willing
    to accept at an auction.
upstage *Theater* Toward the
    back of the stage.
uranic Of the heavens.
ursine Of bears.
ustulation Scorching, burning.
usw Und so weiter *German*
    And so on.
ut infra *Latin* As below.
ut supra *Latin* As above.

ux. Uxor *Latin* Wife.

V

vacillate Stagger, waver in
    opinion or resolution.
vacuity Emptiness.
vacuous Empty, unintelligent.
vade mecum *Latin* Go with me.
vae victus *Latin* Woe to
    the vanquished.
vagary A wild, extravagant
    idea or action.
vainglory Excessive vanity.
valediction Bidding farewell.
valetudenarian An invalid.
valse *French* A waltz.
valuator An appraiser.
vamoose To make off, decamp.
vang A line to steady a gaff
    in a sailing vessel.
vapid Insipid, flat.
vaquero *Spanish* A cowboy.
vasculum A botanist's collect-
    ing box (for specimens).
vatitude Vastness, immensity.
vaticinal Prophetic,
v.d. Various dates.
veer *Nautical* To slacken or
    let out (as chain).
vegetate Live like vegetables.
veld *South Africa* Open land
    with grass and bushes.
velleity Volition in its weak-

est form, not followed by
action. A mere wish.
vellicate To pluck or twitch.
veloce *Music* Very fast.
velours *French* Velvet.
venal Ready to sell one's serv-
ices or influence, glad to
take bribes, unscrupulous.
venatic Of hunting.
vendue A public auction.
venery The sport of hunting and
sexual gratification.
venial Pardonable, not very
wrong.
venire facias *Law* Writ direct-
ing sheriff to summon jury.
venous Of a vein.
ventral Of the belly.
venue *Law* The place where the
jury must be gathered and
the cause tried.
veracious Telling the truth.
verboten *German* Forbidden.
verdant Green with vegetation.
verein *German* Union, society.
verge To incline towards.
verger *British* An attendant
in a church.
veridical Truthful.
verlest Utmost, thoroughgoing.
verisimilitude Appearance or
semblance of truth.
veritable Rightly so called.
vermiform Like a worm.
vernal Of the spring.
verruca A wart.
versant General slope of land.

verso *Printing* The left hand page (of a book).

versus *Latin* Against.

vertex The highest point.

vertiginous Whirling, rotary.

verve *French* Enthusiasm or energy (in artistic or literary work).

very high frequency 30 to 300 megacycles.

vespertine Of the evening.

vespiary A wasps' nest.

vested (a right or interest) subject to no contingency.

vial *British* A small (glass) vessel for liquids.

via media *Latin* A middle way.

vicarious Acting for another.

vice *Latin* Instead of.

vicenary Consisting of twenty.

vide *Latin* See.

videlicet Namely, that is to say, in other words.

viewy Visionary, theorizing.

vigesimal Based on twenty.

vignette A small illustation.

vilify Defame, speak ill of.

vilipend Treat comtemptuously.

villadom *British* Dull people who live in villas.

villatic Of a farm.

villeggiatura *Italian* Stay, retirement in the country.

vinaceous Like wine or grapes.

vincible Not invincible.

vinculum A bond, union or tie.

vindictive Revengeful.

vingt-et-un *French* Twenty one.

vinic Of wine.

vin ordinare *French* Cheap wine
for everyday drinking.

vintner *British* Wine merchant.

violable Able to be violated.

V.I.P. *Airline* Very Important
People (see E.I.P., U.L.P.
& R.A.M.).

viperine Like a viper.

virement *French* The power to
transfer items from one
account to another.

virescent Turning green.

virga Rain that does not
reach the ground.

virgate Shaped like a rod.

virginibus puerisque *Latin*
For girls and boys.

virgin wool Wool that has not
been manufactured.

virgule *Printing* A stroke (/)
between two words meaning
either one or the other.

viridity Greenness, verdancy.

virile Of man (as opposed to
woman or child).

virtu Excellence in objects
of art and the like.

virtue The excess of what you
give to the world over what
you take from it.

virulent Actively poisonous,
malignant, deadly.

vis *Latin* Force.

vis-a-vis *French* Face to face.

viscid Sticky, adhesive.

vis major *Law* Force majeure.

vitellus The yoke of an egg.

vitiate Corrupt, debase, spoil.

viticulture Grape growing.

vitreous Like glass.

vituperation Verbal abuse.

vivandiere *French* A woman who follows a regiment to sell food and drink to soldiers.

viva voce By word of mouth.

vive la bagatelle *French* long live frivolity.

vive valeque *Latin* Live and keep well (used at the end of a letter).

vixen A female fox.

VL Vulgar Latin.

vociferate To shout or bawl.

voila tout *French* That's all.

volation Flying (as birds).

volition Exercise of the will.

volkslied *German* A folk song.

volte-face *French* Turning around to face the other way (in an argument).

volti *Music* Turn the page.

vortiginous Whirling, vortical.

votary One who is bound by a vow (as a monk or nun).

vouchsafe Condescend to grant.

vox *Latin* Voice.

vox barbara *Latin* A barbarous word, as those in botany that are made of elements neither Latin nor Greek.

vox populi *Latin* The voice (or opinion) of the people.

voyageur A Canadian boatman of
    the Hudson's Bay area.
vraisemblance *French* Appear-
    ance of truth.
VSOP *Brandy* Very Suitable
    On Pudding.
vulgar fraction Common fraction.
vulpine Like a fox.

W

wacky Erratic, irrational.
waddy A native Australian
    war club.
wadi *North Africa* A wash,
    usually dry.
wagon-lit *French* A rail-
    road sleeping car.
wainscot *British* Wood on
    the lower part of the
    walls of a room.
wainwright A wagon maker.
waistcoat *British* A vest.
waiver *Law* A deliberate
    relinquishment of some
    right or interest.
walking bass A figure used
    in the bass part of
    boogie-woogie pieces.
walking papers Dismissal.
walkover *Racing* The only
    starter going over the
    course in a walk.
walloper Something inordi-

nately exaggerated.

Walpurgis Night April 30th.

wamble To move uncertainly.

wamus A kind of cardigan.

wanderjahr *German* A workman's year of travel before he settles down.

wantage An amount lacking.

warded Having notches, slots or wards (as in locks).

ward heeler A hanger-on who canvasses voters and does other political chores.

wardroom The dining saloon for officers in a warship.

war paint Full dress, finery.

wash sale Simultaneous buying and selling to give an impression of activity on a stock market (illegal).

washy Diluted too much, weak.

watch night The last night of the year.

waterage *British* Delivery of goods over water routes.

water bottle *British* A canteen.

water closet A flush toilet.

water-inch About 500 cu. ft.

watering place *British* A spa.

watershed *British* A line dividing two drainage areas.

water table The depth below which the ground is saturated with water.

water witching Finding water with a divining rod.

wattage Power in watts.

wattle *British* Stakes interwoven with branches, used to make fences.

wattless An electric current differing in phase by 90 degrees from an associated EMF, or vice versa.

waul To cry like a cat.

wave guide A hollow tube to conduct microwaves.

wax To increase in extent, quantity, power, etc.

waybill A list of goods sent by a common carrier.

wayleave *British* Right of way.

ways and means Ways of raising money for the government.

way train A local train.

WC *British* Water closet.

weariless Tireless, unwearying.

weasel words Intentionally ambiguous statements.

weaver's hitch A sheet bend.

weeper A hired mourner at a funeral.

weft *Weaving* Yarns that interlace with warp, going from selvedge to selvedge.

weir *British* A dam in a river to raise the water.

Weltschmertz *German* Sentimental pessimism.

wether A castrated male sheep.

whacking *British* Very large.

wharfage The use of a wharf.

wherry A light rowboat, skiff.

wheyface A face that is pallid.

whipsaw A narrow blade in a frame, to cut curves.

whistle stop An unimportant town along a railroad.

white damp Carbon monoxide.

whited sepulcher A specious hypocrite.

white dwarf A star of average mass and very small size.

white paper *British* A publication of the House of Commons on a subject.

white slave A white woman who is sold or forced to serve as a prostitute.

whopper A big lie.

wickiup An American Indian hut made with brushwood or covered with mats.

wide *Slang* Knowing, crafty.

wie geht's *German* How goes it? (with you).

Wiener schnitzel *German* A breaded veal cutlet.

wigging *British* A scolding.

wildcat A well drilled in the hope of finding oil.

wilding A wild apple tree.

will-o'-the-wisp Flickering lights, seen over swamps, probably from marsh gas.

wimble *Mining* A device to get rubbish from a bored hole.

wind To signal with a horn.

winder A single one of a winding flight of steps.

wind gap A cut in the upper

part of a mountain ridge.

winding sheet One in which a
corpse is wrapped.

window sash The frame holding
the panes of a window.

wind rose A diagram showing
the frequencies of winds
from various directions.

wind shake A flaw in wood due
the a tree being shaken.

wine gallon 231 cubic inches
(same as a U.S. gallon).

wineglassful Two fluid ounces.

winker *Slang* An eye or lash.

winnow To fan chaff off grain.

winterbourne A channel filled
only when rain is heavy.

winter lambs Those sold before
the 20th of May.

winze *Mining* A small shaft
from one level to another.

wire dancer One who dances or
performs on a high wire.

wireless *British* Radio.

wire pulling Using secret and
unethical influence on a
public official.

wirer One who uses wire to
snare game.

witching Using a divining rod
to find water, etc.

withy *British* A flexible twig.

witling A petty or would-be wit.

wold Open, uncultivated land.

WOG Worthy Oriental Gentleman.

wombat *Australia* A furry animal
that crosses a river by

holding its breath and
walking across the bottom.
wonky *British* Shaky, unsound.
wonted Accustomed.
wood alcohol Methyl alcohol.
wood lot A tract of land set
aside for trees.
wood wool *British* Excelsior.
woof Yarns that go from one selvedge to another in a loom,
interlacing with the warp.
wool fat Lanolin.
wool stapler A dealer in wool.
woozy *Slang* Muddled, confused.
worm fence A snake fence.
wove paper Paper with a plain
surface (unlike laid paper).
wowser *Australian* An excessively puritanical person.
wrack Seaweed used for manure.
wraith An apparition of a living
person, portending death.
wrick Wrench or strain.

X

xenophobia Fear or hatred
of foreigners.

Y

yapp A kind of bookbinding
with a limp leather cover

projecting considerably.
yarborough *Bridge* A hand in
which none of the cards
are higher than nine.
yashmak A veil worn by Moslem
women in public.
yellow jack Quarantine flag.
yellow spot The point of most
acute vision in the retina.
yokefellow Partner, intimate
associate.

Z

zany Like a clown.
zaptiah A Turkish policeman.
zarf Holder for a coffee cup.
zax A tool like an ax, for
cutting roofing slate.
zed *British* The letter 'z'.
zibeline Of the sable.
zingaro *Italian* A Gypsy.
zonda *Spanish* The hot wind of
the Argentine pampas.

CPSIA information can be obtained at www.ICGtesting.com
Printed in the USA
BVOW030901081011

273124BV00001B/130/P

9 781462 035007